D0027445

	DATE DUE		

BOMBAY SMILES

JAUME SANLLORRENTE

TRANSLATED FROM THE SPANISH BY
Gwendollyn Gout AND *Robert Dreesen*

PAUL DRY BOOKS
Philadelphia 2009

First Paul Dry Books edition, 2009

Paul Dry Books, Inc.
Philadelphia, Pennsylvania
www.pauldrybooks.com

Printed in the United States of America

Author's note: The names of certain individuals and organizations
have been changed to protect their privacy.

All photographs courtesy of Sonrisas de Bombay.
Cover photograph © Llibert Teixido, 2007.

Library of Congress Cataloging-in-Publication Data

Sanllorente, Jaume, 1976–
  [Sonrisas de Bombay. English]
  Bombay smiles / Jaume Sanllorrente ; translated from the Spanish
by Gwendollyn Gout and Robert Dreesen. — 1st Paul Dry Books ed.
     p. cm.
  ISBN 978-1-58988-055-9 (alk. paper)
  1. Orphans—India. 2. Child prostitution—India. 3. India—
Social conditions. 4. Sanllorente, Jaume, 1976– —Travel—India.
5. Journalists—Spain—Biography. I. Title.
  HV1292.S2613 2009
  362.730954—dc22

                                                           2009026240

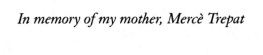

In memory of my mother, Mercè Trepat

Wherever there is a bit of colour, a note of song, a grace of form, there comes the call for our love.

—RABINDRANATH TAGORE

CONTENTS

BOMBAY SMILES

To live is to remember to forget.
Forgive what you must forgive.
Forget what you must forget.
Embrace life with renewed strength . . .
We must be able to see each moment with fresh eyes,
like a flower that has just opened.

—MATA AMRITANANDAMAYI

I'm grabbing this calm moment to finish writing the story you're about to read. The story, the beginning, the successes . . . everything seems a dream now, mingled with the shouts and laughter of children playing in the garden just outside my window. Yet parts of the story, the dark times, sometimes seem like a nightmare. It depends on what's happening around me at the moment. Right now I feel at peace, as if an oasis of tranquility existed within the garden walls beyond the white curtains of my room. Even some of the leaks in the ceiling caused by the monsoons have dried up.

1

Yet I know I am suspending my disbelief. The past is eternally present, the present eternally the future. A child's laughter isn't to be taken for granted.

I was asked to write this book by Jordi Nadal of Plataforma Editorial, a publisher in Barcelona. He had contacted Bombay Smiles' press representative after watching one of my lectures on video. I spoke on that occasion about the colors of this world's wall, about its darkness and about our responsibility to transform that darkness into an unblemished white. If some of us paint a small white patch there will be less of a black wall. If every one of us paints a patch of that wall, it will eventually be entirely white.

"Jaume, you have to agree," the rep said to me after Mr. Nadal contacted her. "You *will* write a book about your experience, won't you?"

"What? I think it is way too soon to do that," I replied. "It's not the time to write a book. Especially with all the work I have here . . ."

"How often have you told your story?" she asked. "You just have to write it down!"

She was right, and so I wrote. I had often tried to tell the story, to get it on paper, yet it never came out as I wanted it to. Piles of paper filled with notes and thoughts lay in the corner of my office, grimy from

Prologue

Bombay's dust and pollution; smelling of incense smoke from the temples and of cardamom from the chai that I liked so much. My papers reek of the pestilence that fills the narrow alleys of the slums, of musty bandages dampened by the leprosy of innocent bodies. Both my writings and the paper on which I wrote reflect my daily life here in Bombay. My notebooks are filled with dreams, some of which became reality. Yes, I am surrounded by paper—not just my story, but briefings and project proposals, plans, calendars . . . all in order and ready for revision.

As I run my hand over the pile of dreams, as I absorb my experiences from the past few years, I tell myself that the practical papers would not exist if the pile of dreams had not come true. I close my eyes and open myself through my fingers, to all those memories. I let those memories circle my soul, touching every organ and leaving an aroma, sometimes sweet, other times bitter.

This is my story. It takes place in a magic land of lively colors and smiles, of coincidences coalescing into destiny. Not everything is here, because silences are also part of this peaceful struggle against poverty, one that continues, one to which I've devoted my life.

The room seems warm and friendly now as I gaze at the flaking lime-yellow walls surrounding me, the scene of interminable meetings and sleepless nights. These walls, too, have witnessed successes that at first seemed failures; happy moments where only sadness had been known; solidarity and adversity, controversy, and a thousand conversations—sometimes with other people.

I am alone now. No teacher is asking for a raise; no neighbor complaining that an orphanage for untouchables is unacceptable; no architect showing blueprints for the schools; no secretary handing me letters from Spain, letters I have waited for, for a thousand nights. Not even my loyal assistant, Vinay, is around, thanking me for the job that allows his children to eat; even the guards, to whom I have yet to get accustomed, are absent now.

There is nobody, and yet the room is full of presences. There is the universe of which those children and their laughter in the garden are part, and of which I am part. There are the papers, my past. Soon it will be dark, but first the miracle.

I open the curtains on the enormous window that has provided so much comfort over these past few years, my window to the Soul. Everyday I receive the generous gift of sunset: the sky with its beautiful yellow shades turning pink, then mauve blue, all leading toward the imposing mystery of the star-filled night. How beautiful the universe is.

Prologue

I contemplate the universe as if it were a movie screen. What would have happened if the script, my script, those children's script, had ended abruptly? What would this screen reveal now? I quickly discard those thoughts and focus once again on the sunset.

The little ones are still laughing as they watch a boy with a big head and jet black eyes climb a tree in search of an out-of-season mango. I wish everything were like this, always, I think to myself. I know it's not possible. Behind the vines growing on the garden walls is a city. I may die here one day. Much work and living remains, however. This city and its people changed my destiny and the destiny of many others. This city, this place, this time . . . my destiny, their destiny . . .

Jaume Sanllorente
Bombay, August 2007

ONE

A VACATION

We should know at every moment that life is not about being free, because we already are free. Any idea about having ties is an illusion. Any idea about being happy or unhappy is a great illusion. —Swami Vivekananda

My flight to India departed very early. I had worked that night at the restaurant, so I slept for only a couple of hours before taking a taxi to El Prat airport at four-thirty in the morning. "You are my Guinness Book of World Record for airport fares," the cab driver told me. "No one has ever asked me to go to the airport this early."

I had a leisurely breakfast at a bar before checking in. I've always liked airports; they are perfect for observing people. Where are they going, all those people? Where are they coming from? And why are they traveling? Some are searching for what they will never find; others for what they have already found but don't know it; still others will find what they are searching for, but it will be too late. And of course some are traveling simply to go, while others are seeking better luck in a distant city, or looking for someone to love and be loved by.

We are always looking for new lives, for escapes. We are always seeking what we don't have, and what we have we are unhappy with. All these searches end in the same place. Whatever my reasons for going or coming, for fleeing, a part of my soul stays in every place I've been: a distant memory—a smell or song—remains with us, bringing pain or pleasure, or both, for the rest of our lives and allows us to live once more those moments in a day or week when we experienced life intensely and purely.

I thought again about my trip and reviewed my itinerary, writing it down in a little notebook. I would first stop in Amman, Jordan, to see the capital before catching another flight to Delhi. I liked the idea of traveling by myself, perhaps because I am an only child. I know that I am alone in this world. I know it and I am comfortable with it. I am easy in my solitude.

I don't remember the details of the flight, but it went well, like so many other flights: sleep, turbulence, read, eat, more turbulence, and so forth. Amman was wonderful. I met four charming Spanish girls who were on their way to India with the same tour operator I was using. I smiled to myself because they reminded me of the travel agents who had helped me book my tickets to India. I recall being quite ambivalent about a vacation at the time.

ONE COULD SAY I had everything: work, family, friends, youth . . . I liked my life and wasn't looking for change, yet my hectic schedule was taking its toll. I was a journalist during the day, working for an economics magazine. I routinely wrote articles about international trade, market analysis, port movements, agreements and partnerships in the transportation system, and logistics. I had finished my journalism studies without knowing what I wanted to do, and landed my job by chance. I learned to appreciate the work despite boring conferences and equally boring power struggles among directors. And there was always the tension I faced when actually writing my articles—what to include and what to omit.

Had it not been for my asthma attacks, which became more frequent, I might have continued with my hectic schedule. Soon it became clear, however, especially to my colleagues and friends, that I needed a vacation. Yes, I would go to Africa, somewhere south of the Sahara. I was intensely interested in black Africa's political situation ever since I wrote a brief thesis in college about Rwanda's genocide and international responsibility. I had read countless articles and books about the history of many of those countries, especially those situated around the Great Lakes.

It had been years since I last took a vacation, so I had enough money for an extended stay. One morning, after a long night's work, I walked into the first travel agency I could find. The young people inside were amiable, and I immediately grew fond of them.

"What can we do for you?" they asked.

"Well, I have some vacation time and I don't have a particular destination. I feel like going to Africa, but I don't really care if I go elsewhere. I mean, it's also OK if it's the United States or Scandinavia," I replied.

The three of us laughed. Marta, Ramon, and I quickly understood each other. We didn't settle on a destination that day, but I returned to their office several times throughout the week; always we talked and laughed, and talked some more. They were excellent at their jobs, and kind. Marta introduced me to Raja yoga, which is considered to be a good practice for inner concentration. She and I went to meditation sessions several times.

One day Ramon asked, "Why not India? You would love it. I've been there and really like it. I can talk to you about the places I know and the friends I have there."

I was horrified. "India," I said. "I'm sure it's beautiful, but the truth is I don't feel like going. I have been told that it's so filthy, that there's so much poverty . . . I don't know, it really doesn't appeal to me."

"I also think that you would like it," added Marta. "You're interested in yoga, and yoga comes from there."

"No," I replied, "I'm not going there. I'm not a hippie who wants to go to India to 'find myself' or anything like that."

The Spanish writer and philosopher Miguel Unamuno said that those who travel do so either to find their destiny or to flee the place they come from. Neither applied to me, yet somehow Marta and Ramon convinced me to go to India. And so I bought a tourist package called "India with Liberty," which would take me to Rajasthan and down to Benares. India would be my destination.

"IN A FEW MINUTES we will land in Delhi." Who wouldn't be woken up by such words? Who wouldn't anticipate? What if I didn't like it? What if I got tired of the place in the first week and wanted to leave?

"Flight attendants, disarm the doors . . ." My anticipation grew.

When the plane's doors opened, I remained seated to avoid the frenzy that accompanies exits from airplanes. How little I know about India, I thought. "How could I have come to a country in which I have so little interest? What the hell am I doing?" As I crossed the plane's threshold, I was met by hot and fetid air and an indescribable smell that accompanied me for the remainder of the trip. How bad this country smells, I thought. What unpleasant heat. After I claimed my luggage, which involved confusion after confusion, I took a van to my hotel near Connaught Place, one of the principal axes in Delhi, and among the most crowded. It was around eight o'clock in the evening, and the street was packed with people, even though it was dark. I couldn't see in the glaring lights that emanated from what seemed like millions of small businesses. I couldn't breathe because of the incomparable human congestion: I had never seen so many people in one place, not even in my imagination.

After arriving at my hotel, I explored the neighborhood. I didn't like what I saw. The ground was full of red spots—I later discovered they were gobs of *paan*, a chewable herb to which many Indians are addicted, not so dissimilar from the addiction of Westerners to tobacco. I couldn't walk freely, swinging my arms and expanding my gate, but instead had to jostle and shuffle.

I was deeply moved by the abandoned and malnourished dogs. Their ribs showed through mangy coats; some had open wounds where flesh and bone could be seen. All seemed beaten down, not just physically but spiritually. I learned later that dogs are ill-treated in India because Hindus believe they are reincarnations of thieves or other reprehensible people.

Not only the dogs wore desperate looks; so did the people. The poverty was staggering: people sleeping in the street, begging, looking at me with desperate eyes. And children, hundreds of children half naked, playing with trash or some dead animal. Suddenly I saw a cow strolling toward me, as if it were walking down the trail in a pasture, heading toward the barn to be milked. My amusement didn't last long—the pain was visible everywhere, and all around the sights caused me to despair.

I hadn't expected all this pain and misery. My friends at the travel agency in Barcelona certainly hadn't said anything about it. Though I had no expectations before arriving in India, it wouldn't have surprised me if I

BOMBAY SMILES

had found the entire scene so disgusting that I got on a plane the next day and returned to Spain. Truth be told, I did want to get out of there as soon as possible. It was too much. I was overwhelmed, and that overwhelming feeling followed me into the night. I couldn't sleep. All I could think about was the pain out there and what I was going to do for a month. How could this place, this time, be part of the same world that I came from? Was this reality or a nightmare? I felt as if I had been transported to the Middle Ages.

Journalists would later say, in articles about me and my experiences, that I fell in love with India at first sight. The truth is that I disliked the country immensely at the beginning. How could I fall in love with misery?

In time I would come to understand that I had undergone a sort of metamorphosis that first night. I've often compared the experience to a puzzle. The pieces of my inner puzzle, which could also be called my soul, were floating around, unattached, leaving a gaping hole. They would be put back together, in time, in another configuration. Was it true that India changed one's values? Such statements are usually clichés.

The next day my tour group traveled to Jaipur— a beautiful city shrouded in what seemed to be fog but was, in fact, pollution. Yet even such pervasive pollution didn't poison my increasing enjoyment. That first night's anguish began to recede, and my curiosity began to grow. I bought books to deepen my knowledge of Hinduism and the caste system. I began to read about the continent in particular and humanity in general.

I loved Mandawa, another town in Rajasthan, which was full of charm. I slept at a former maharaja's palace that had been converted into a hotel. From the tallest tower one could look into the vast desert, the view obstructed only by the bright colors of a beautiful sari elegantly moving forward in a sea of sand.

Next came Agra, where I spent hours contemplating the spectacular beauty of the Taj Mahal, the largest monument ever built for love. This amazing Mogul building, which I visited from early in the morning until dusk, was built by Shah Jahan as a mausoleum for his second wife, Mumtaz Mahal, who died in childbirth in 1631. More than eighteen thousand people are said to have worked on the construction. After the monument was finished, they cut off the arms of some of the workers to avoid a repetition of such perfection.

"We all, somehow, build our own Taj Mahal," said my guide. "Do you know what yours is, sir?"

"I don't," I replied instantly. "But I'm convinced it will be related to love as well."

His question made me think. My answer made me wince. Did I really believe that? What would my Taj Mahal be? Had I created something already? Was I setting the right foundation for my life? Did my relationships—with my family and friends, with loved ones—represent a structure as impressive as the Taj Mahal?

The Taj Mahal will always be part of my life, as it is part of the lives of those who have seen it. Yet the place that most impressed me during that trip was Benares (Varanasi). This sacred city, known as the "City of Light," is believed to belong to the god Shiva. They say that the Ganges River, which traverses the city, flows from Shiva's hair.

I enjoyed strolling through the narrow streets surrounding the *ghats*—stone steps built in the eighteenth century that descend to the river, and where thousands of pilgrims pray. One of the most fabulous moments was an outing on a small boat on the Ganges at sunrise. The sun seemed so close, so impressive, so orange. I could touch it, I thought. How lucky am I to be here. Yes, something had been altered. And whenever something is altered within one's self, that alteration is manifest: one's perceptions change and then one's actions change. Indeed, the "world," one's own world, changes.

A Vacation

I was still caught unawares by certain sights, however, still shocked out of comfortable Western life. For example, I was shocked by "dying huts," which lined certain streets—small caves or clay huts, exposed to onlookers, that families rented for loved ones who were dying. Hindus believe that earthly life is constituted by cycles, and thus one dies and is reborn in a process called *samsara*. The quality of reincarnation is determined by *karma*—one's behavior in one's previous life. Obeying one's *dharma* (duty) in this life guarantees a better existence in the next life. Conversely, bad behavior, or karma, will cause a person to be reincarnated as a member of an inferior caste, or even as a dog.

During this time I met Devi, an old woman accompanied by her two sons. She had come to die next to the Ganges. Her eyes radiated love despite being clouded and virtually enshrouded. They were almost pure white. I looked into those eyes, or rather was drawn into her gaze, and remembered an old poem that I've always liked, by an American named Henry Van Dyke (1852–1933):

Time is
Too slow for those who wait,
too swift for those who fear,

17

too long for those who grieve,
too short for those who rejoice.
But for those who love,
time is eternity.

The spirit of that last line . . . her eyes, she knew more than most of us will ever know. She *knew* in her agony, at eighty-three, in a "death hut" in Varanasi, that another life was awaiting her. She had already closed her eyes to this life. I will remember this woman, for reasons different from those for which I will remember the Taj Mahal.

I was also impressed by the funeral pyres, by the burning of the dead. Some tourists were horrified by the scene, yet the Hindu funerary ritual is among the most beautiful rites (of any kind) that I've ever seen.

When I wasn't observing the pyres, I loved to sit on the steps of some *ghat* and observe the *sadhus*—men who have left everything, who have renounced their families and wives, their social positions; men who have given up all material possessions to embark on a spiritual journey through meditation and the study of sacred texts.

Could I do this, renounce everything and everyone? I didn't think so. I felt attached to my room and my clothes, to my small boxes of memories. I liked my job, and I liked my life. I remembered the times working in the restaurant, which I did to supplement my income from journalism. My weekend occupation meant tending to celebrities in one of the best neighborhoods in Barcelona. Musicians, politicians, princes and princesses, aristocrats (real ones and impostors), and an unending list of characters constituting the world's social cream of the crop visited the restaurant. My job was to solve "problems," to get irritated clients to leave with a smile, to make everyone comfortable. I handled reservations, not taking them, but greeting the clientele, knowing their favorite tables, knowing how they liked to be treated . . . I liked this job and couldn't imagine giving it up for a place like India.

I have wonderful memories of those times working in the restaurant. My colleagues and I talked and gossiped for hours. We spent many nights laughing and crying, putting up with the petulance and whims of customers so we could make ends meet. I never got bored. Many days I got by on two hours of sleep. I knew that the feverish rhythm and high pitch wouldn't last forever. Like many people in states of transition, I existed between illusion and expectancy.

But did I need that life? Was it possible I only thought that I liked my life? Such questions continu-

19

ally emerged amid the changes that were coming over me there in India, on that trip—each object, each gesture and sight inspired questions about my existence, about the choices I made, about my entire life. Probably like many human beings, I've always been fascinated by individuals who, upon learning that they have only a short time to live, change their lives, give away material possessions, and begin to really live; people who begin to value being over having. So often I've asked, Why don't more of us do it? Why don't we live as if we're about to die, as if we have a short time to live? In fact, our time on earth is short, so why don't we live more deliberately?

At that moment, observing the *sadhus*, I knew I was less free than I had thought. I knew that I had built a prison for myself and that I alone possessed the power to bend its bars, to free myself. Varanasi affected me profoundly. It was there that I witnessed the essence of India. Later I also realized that, like many tourists, I had fallen victim to the city's most common scam, "firewood for the poor." Someone offers to show you the funerary pyres and remains with you for the duration of your visit. Then, at the end, he informs you that some people cannot afford firewood for their pyres and that a contribution would be welcomed, a balm for the pain of not having enough money to pay for one's own immolation. And I fell for it. Of course the money often isn't for firewood to burn the impoverished dead, but to line some guide's pocket.

When I went to bed on my last evening in Varanasi, I felt a tickling in my legs. The next night the tickling became more acute, and a couple of days later it had turned into an unbearable itch that broke out in sores. I've always joked that my body is a five-star hotel for illnesses. Fungus, allergies, asthma, infections, suppurations, viruses . . . I've had them all. And I knew this ailment was scabies, no doubt about it. The next day I went to a pharmacy and asked for a lotion with permetrine, a substance that kills parasites and their eggs. It worked. I mention this seemingly innocuous event because it was preparation—destiny's joke, if you will—for the multiple attacks of scabies and infections I would suffer in the future.

FROM VARANASI I flew to Nepal, a country much cleaner than India, which I immediately liked. Unfortunately I didn't have time to visit any of the schools established by Vicki Sherpa (Victoria Subirana), a Catalan woman who, many years earlier, had decided to settle in Nepal and educate impoverished children. Her humanitarian work is legendary and inspiring.

I did, however, visit Maiti Nepal, the first non-governmental organization (NGO) that I contacted in Asia. I had never been interested in such organizations, which made me feel a bit guilty. How could I not have been interested in people who work to make this a better world? I began to realize I had been immersed in a kind of egotistical indifference with respect to the rest of the planet. "A pimple on our nose sometimes obsesses us more than the fact that each day many children die of hunger in the world," says a Chinese proverb.

The founder of Maiti Nepal is Anuradha Koirala, with whom I had the pleasure to talk at length. This energetic and charismatic woman rescues Nepalese women who have been kidnapped by prostitution rings. Once again I asked myself whether I would be able to make such a sacrifice. Did I have the courage to do what this woman was doing?

Anuradha told me that many girls are sold by their own families to prostitution rings in neighboring countries, India, for example. The girls are sexually exploited until they are overcome by some illness, and then are left to die in the street.

"Where do they work? Where are the brothels?" I asked.

A Vacation

"Most are taken to Kamathipura, Bombay's red-light district," Anuradha explained.

"Bombay . . ." I repeated, wondering why I hadn't included that city on my tour. "I would have liked to go to Bombay, Mrs. Koirala, but now it's probably too late since I have no intention of returning to India. I like the country a lot, but not enough to go back."

TWO

BOMBAY

The human voice will never be able to travel as far as the tiny and silent voice of conscience. —GANDHI

Krishnamurti once wrote that we think our suffering is personal, that we are closed to the suffering of humanity. I now reflect back to my friend's death and how much suffering it caused me. His name was Carl Berrisford, and he was from London. In Barcelona we used to go to the Magic Fountain. He loved the sound and light show. We looked at it, we laughed, and we talked amusedly about the spectacular beauty of the Spanish girls, dark and perfumed, looking like princesses in a Hindu fairy tale.

One cold day while having lunch with some friends next to the sea, I received news that Carl had been hit by a subway train in London. He was in a coma, and he died before I arrived in London to see him in the hospital. I hope he is now in a heaven of colorful fountains, marveling at the beautiful, dark-haired girls for eternity. I visit those fountains every year in homage to my friend. The last time was just before I booked my vacation to India.

There were thousands of stars in the sky that March night. The Mediterranean was calm and conveyed a sense of peace as it caressed my feet. Behind me, the Mapfre Towers—the unmistakable symbols of Barcelona and the Olympics—imposed themselves on the city. It is like a postcard, I thought, though only later would I learn that the secret is to look at a postcard, not as if it were outside of oneself, but to be a part of it, to *be* the postcard. It is not about observing a painting, but about being one of the pigments in the painting. It is the difference between being and knowing.

Sitting on the beach and listening to the sea that night I was seized with sensation, with longing. In literary or philosophical terms this feeling has often been described as "the nostalgia for what is yet to come." A restless evening had just ended. The Rolling Stones and their retinue had been in the restaurant. After leaving work, I rode my motorcycle around Barcelona, toward the Montjuïc fountains. I liked to ride along the Gran Via, Marina Street, the Diagonal, and observe the city at different times of the day.

I do not know very well why or how—and I could not explain it rationally—but some months after my trip to India I found myself begging my boss for a four-week vacation so I could return. My reasons for wanting to go back might have been related to that nostalgia for the future. The months following my first trip were bizarre. I had much trouble returning to daily life. My mind wandered the Rajasthan's deserts and Varanasi's narrow streets, returning ever so often to Barcelona's tidy sidewalks. As I mentioned earlier, it's not that I fell in love with the country, quite the opposite, but it seeped into my soul and I couldn't forget it.

BACK IN BARCELONA after my first trip to India, I bought books on Hinduism, Jainism, Buddhism, Sikhism, Zoroastrianism, and many other religions found in that country of a thousand beliefs. I immersed myself in political history and read several biographies of Mahatma Gandhi, of Indira Gandhi, the iron woman of the East, and of Dr. B. R. Ambedkar, among the greatest champions of the untouchables. I analyzed travelers' accounts describing the land that had ceased to be foreign to me. I devoured essays by Swami Vivekananda, Rabindranath Tagore, and other Indian philosophers, all exuding wisdom.

I couldn't ride my motorcycle through the streets of Barcelona or walk around without being accompanied by a quote or thought from one of these great minds. I found myself committing their words to memory or suddenly discovering that I had already done so through countless recitations. A new lesson emerged with each recall. I realized how ignorant I was, how little I understood. The main thing I learned, in general, was that in Indian philosophy the soul and universe replace individuals and personalities.

Numerous quotes, from Vivekananda especially, became embedded in my memory:

> All of Good and Evil's responsibility is within you.
> It is a great fountain of hope. What you have done
> you can undo.

And so I returned to India to undo what I had done, landing in a city whose name I had heard only once before, in a song by the Spanish band Mecano. In Mecano's song, Bombay is a paradise.

Bombay is the financial and commercial center of India. It was established around the second century B.C., when Koli fishermen began inhabiting the various islands that now form the city. It was governed by different Indian dynasties before it came under the rule of the Arabs and, later, Portuguese, who handed it over to the sultan of Gujarat in 1534. The British government took control of Bombay in 1665, although it was soon sold to the East India Company for ten pounds per year.

In 1996 Bombay's name was changed to Mumbai, a Marathi name (Marathi is the dialect spoken in the state of Maharashtra) that comes from the goddess Mumba, worshiped by the early fishermen who inhabited the city. The great Marathi hero Chhatrapati Shivaji had the power and strength to pull together the Maharashtra state, of which Bombay is the current capital. Some political parties today, like Shiv Sena, are fervent followers of Shivaji—they are tooth-and-nail champions of everything concerning the state and Hinduism, their religion.

Bombay is the epicenter of the massive Bollywood film industry, the largest maker of movies in the world. As with California and Hollywood, to which countless Americans flock seeking stardom, their first break, or simply a piece of the action, so with Bombay and Bollywood. Thousands of Indians arrive every year in search of a dream, which in many cases degenerates into a nightmare of extortion and exploitation.

When I arrived in Bombay, the heat did not startle me as it had on my earlier trip; now it seemed friendlier, less foreign. Even so, I was still met with a blast almost beyond description, and it was early morning. I had left this country thinking I would never come back, yet here I was descending the plane's steps. I took a prepaid taxi and rode across the entire city to the south district, where I would stay. My hotel was in the Colaba neighborhood. The hotel, which had been recommended, had a very good quality-to-price ratio and was near the Gateway of India, a monument built to commemorate the visit of King George V in 1911.

At that hour there was little light, and during the cab ride I noticed gray objects extending into the street on both sides of the car. I soon discovered that these were people sleeping there because they had nowhere else to go. The new Mumbai seemed gray to me, dark shades of solitude, of filth and poverty, a very sad color indeed. That was Bombay's color—gray sadness.

After a few days of looking around, I took a bus to the small state of Goa. I stayed for a weekend in a small wooden cabin in the middle of the Benaulim district, which is very quiet. How beautiful it was. Each morning I was awakened by the sound of the sea's waves, only to gaze at the beautiful forms created by clouds and the attractive immensity of the Arabian Sea.

I then took a bus to Bangalore, making my way down to the Anantapur region so that I could visit the projects of the Vicente Ferrer Foundation. When I arrived, Vicente and Anna Ferrer gave me a warm welcome. Thus began an inspiring experience that would manifest itself in numerous surprises later on. What happened next seemed a fairly innocuous train ride back to Bombay. Yet that rusty wagon was not taking me to just another city, it was taking me to the rest of my life —it was the journey of the rest of my life.

The capital of Maharashtra seemed to me exactly as it had appeared on the night of my first arrival: horrendous—full of dust and pollution, saturated with people. I constantly bumped into *them*: Filthy, lice-ridden, starving and rickety, they besieged me with their penetrating eyes that seemed to intensify each moment with all the injustices inflicted on them by an unjust society. They were the untouchables—picking up garbage, begging, praying for clemency in the kingdom of ignorance, and victimized by absurd laws, by those "above" them, by the wealthy.

There were so many poor people. Wasn't Mumbai supposed to be the Mecca of Bollywood, the urban center of big business and dreams? Wasn't Calcutta supposed to be the worst place in India? Foreigners concentrated in Colaba, the tourist center of the city. Most travelers pass through Colaba on the way to Goa and Kerala, or other destinations in the South.

Bombay tormented me day and night. I was besieged by the same anguish and pain I had felt on that first night in Delhi. Once again I was gripped by a strange sense of responsibility amid ignorance and misery. And yet other shifts were occurring, too. I remember a pretty scene, one seemingly without significance, yet unforgettable. It was about noon when the taxi in which I was traveling stopped at one of the many cross streets of Marine Drive, called "the Queen's Necklace." At night, the lights along the curve of the bay appear like a bright diamond choker.

Just in front of one of the most popular live music clubs in the city, an old woman with a hypnotic smile approached my window. Her eyes shone with goodness, and her dark face was deeply and nobly traced by years, as well as sorrow and solitude, no doubt. She was selling roses, fresh and intensely red, as intense as her face.

"Buy a rose from me, I pray you," she said with a honeyed voice. "Your girlfriend will be happy."

"Madam, I don't have a girlfriend," I responded.

"Well I can be your girlfriend then," she said sweetly, still smiling.

The tenderness of that woman made such a deep impression that I bought the whole bunch from her and added enough extra rupees to buy many more bunches. Her expression of joy was a beautiful gift, and I was surprised by the happiness I felt in the thought of her jubilation. I felt such pleasure, the pleasure of giving without expecting anything in return.

To MAKE OTHERS happy is the secret of happiness; there is no other trick. That's it. That's all. We must concentrate on others, on how to make other people happy. If we do that, we don't need to buy self-help books or go outside of ourselves seeking pleasure. Our humanity comes from other human beings; therefore our happiness must come from serving others, from serving other human beings. It is the indisputable formula for the meaning of our existence, to dance to the true compass of humanity and life. We are instruments of love, and instruments are only worthwhile and significant when we let them guide us, when we listen to them.

It seems to me that we are always seeking happiness in the wrong places, from the wrong things. We expect to be happier if only we have this or buy that, if only we live in this or another way—measuring ourselves against others in an effort to reach our own fulfillment. We are wrong. Only if we forget our own interests and ambitions, and focus on the needs of others will we be able to understand and fully inhabit happiness with all its notes and nuances.

We should consider ourselves a window pane, looking through it to the beyond, fixing on beautiful horizons that lie beyond the pane. The further our gaze goes beyond the window, the further we leave behind our egotistical goals. To seek happiness in things, for example, is to become the window pane and not the horizon. What value does a shirt have that hangs in the closet? What is the use of a telephone if there is nobody to talk to? Just as a shirt is for dressing someone, so we should dress the hearts and souls of others with gifts and glee, and pass on the joy of life through love.

THE RED LIGHT turned green (it is one of the few that are respected in the city), and the taxi moved away. I tried to give the roses back to the woman (they were for my girlfriend and she was my girlfriend), but the flowers flew all over the place, forming a pretty red cloud in the middle of the dusty city. The landscape behind me was indescribable: the smiling old woman, red petals dancing around her, arms waving, people watching. I was profoundly thankful for the experience, for being able to help someone in need—of a full stomach or a decent bed. And yet I was unsatisfied; I was unhappy. Why should I be happy because I helped someone to a meal? Why should I be happy because an old woman has a better cardboard box on which to sleep?

THREE

POOJA

> Poverty shouldn't exist in a civilized society, it should be confined to museums. And that's where it will go. When schoolchildren visit the museums of poverty with their teachers, they will be horrified to witness the suffering and humiliation that human beings were subjected to. They will blame their ancestors for having tolerated that inhumane situation and for allowing it to be so extensive among populations until the first part of the 21st century. —MUHAMMAD YUNUS

The new places I discovered in Bombay passed as quickly as the days, yet the hustle and bustle didn't bother me any longer. I had gotten used to the frenetic rhythm of the place, to devouring delicious *vada pavs*, a mixture of potatoes and spices served inside a piece of bread. They are known as the "Indian hamburgers." I enjoyed *pav bhaji*, cooked in the small restaurants of Juhu, and I kept in my memory every image and situation I witnessed.

Despite all the extraordinary experiences I was having, my soul was being eaten away by the poverty in Bombay. I couldn't get used to seeing luxury hotels and new cars next to hundreds of half-naked children—their faces full of scabs, their bodies full of infections—begging on the streets. I saw these children, who were destined to be seen by so many as weeds in the garden of life, as beautiful flowers.

One afternoon after visiting Mani Bhavan, where Gandhi stayed when he visited Bombay between 1917 and 1934, I took a taxi back to my hotel. The taxi driver got lost (so he said, probably to take advantage of a tourist lost in thought) and drove through a district crumbling with shacks. On each side of the road wide extensions of tin roofs could be seen, stretching to the horizon. I wanted to plunge into this sea of misery even though I knew of its daunting depths. Indeed, I sensed that I would find pleasant realities in its farthest reaches.

Darkness was descending and I knew that it was too late to visit the City Museum.

Suddenly, like destiny's accomplice, traffic engulfed us. We were locked in smog and sewage. "Where are we?" I asked.

"Matunga, Sir. All of this is Dharavi, a slum district."

I asked the driver to let me out. I paid and began walking down the road until it met the gray sea. I noticed a girl with a beautiful face sitting on a small mound of the slope near the road, looking at me and smiling. As I walked toward her, I thought she would run away or simply ignore me. Instead, she stared intently at me, her smile broadening the closer I approached.

"What is your name?" I asked in English.

"My name is Pooja," she answered.

"You speak very good English!"

"Yes, I speak English at work."

I turned my head and noticed several children begging alongside cars piling on the road—slaves to unending traffic in the city. I understood then what Pooja did for a living and was surprised that she didn't ask for money.

"Where do you live, Pooja?"

"Here, very near. Do you want to see my house? I live there with my parents and my brother. Come, I'll show you."

She took my hand without hesitation, and together we entered a narrow street, about three feet wide, that crossed the slums. Pooja walked lightly without looking ahead. Her gaze was fixed on me and she studied the veins in my hand. She tried to imitate my gait and match my pace. She was dirty and disheveled, smiling from ear to ear, either thinking about the afternoon of games to be had with her friends or the benefits she would reap from this encounter. She had no shoes. She was wearing a worn pale green t-shirt and a graceful maroon full skirt with small white flowers on its bottom edge. The skirt gave her a festive air despite the landscape of waste surrounding her.

Matunga is part of Dharavi, one of Bombay's enormous slum districts. Twenty million inhabitants, about 60 percent of the city's population, live in minuscule huts made of cardboard, asbestos, and other, more harmful, materials. Dharavi is the largest slum district in Asia and one of the most extended in the world, along with the suburbs of Johannesburg in South Africa and the shanty towns of Rio de Janeiro in Brazil.

"We will be there soon," Pooja kept saying, always smiling.

To our left, next to the back wall of a train station, some children were screaming with joy while playing cricket. To our right, omnipresent rats scurried among stones, ferns, and garbage. Pooja's skin was quite dark compared to the other children's. Her big, sparkling black eyes were slanted, and when she smiled two horizontal furrows formed that seemed like ink rivulets.

"I live here." She pointed at a shack made of wood, asbestos, and rusty corrugated iron.

An enormous cardboard door was tied with wires to the asbestos wall. Outside were piles of bags of garbage, to be sold to recycling companies; this is how most of the slum's inhabitants earn a living.

I stuck my head through the door. It was tiny of course, about ten square feet, and dark. There were two filthy mattresses with holes all over, probably caused by rats. The mattresses were folded against a gray shelf on which were cooking items, very well organized, and a television covered with a filthy rug. Here was Pooja's home.

Suddenly I felt someone's hand on my back. I turned and I saw a beautiful woman with a symmetrical face and a kind expression. She must have been thirty years old going on fifty. I understood from Pooja's excitement —she was jumping up and down—that this was her mother. She talked to me but I didn't understand a word of Hindi, so I could only smile. Everyone was smiling, and only later did I come to realize how ubiquitous smiles are in that world, and how sustaining they are.

"She says that you should sit down, she will bring something to drink," said Pooja, pointing to a bed of grass rope tied to four wood bases.

"No, please, tell her not to bother." I was thinking about the economic strain a can of soda means for these people. Pooja and I talked while her mother was in the corner.

"America?" she asked curiously.

"No, I am from Spain."

"Spain," she repeated, looking to the side and pretending that she knew what I was talking about.

"How many people live here?" I asked.

"Nine—my mother, my father, my older brother, his wife, their baby, my sister, me, my grandmother, and my uncle. We don't all fit inside the house, so we also sleep outside."

I remembered the gray bundles that I had seen from my taxi that first night in Bombay.

Soon, two women with beautiful pink and orange saris and jasmine posies in their hair approached and offered a bottle of Thums Up, the Indian Coca-Cola. How much we have to learn from such people, I thought; how India requires so much humility and generosity, how both suffuse the lives of the poor. Would they be as generous if they suddenly became rich? While sitting there, I began to question the value of money and its perverse effects. On the other hand, with just a bit of money, Pooja and her family could have a house large enough for everyone to sleep in, albeit in close quarters. This hut probably crumbles with each monsoon's rain, I thought. At what level does money cease to be a necessity and become a social poison?

As I was finishing my delicious Thums Up, we heard a spine-chilling scream. Pooja and her mother, as well as the ladies who had offered me the drink and whose eyes were fixed on me, quickly rose and ran outside. Across the way, a man was beating a woman. Despite her pleas, he landed blow after blow on her face and body; even from that distance I could see the fury and murder in his bloodshot eyes.

Pooja ran over and hugged a frightened child crying next to the woman. Men were standing calmly by as if they were watching a friend fix the sewer. Meanwhile several women were trying to protect the victim with their screams. I reacted strongly to the scene and made my way over, only to be forcefully stopped by a strong young man.

While trying to free myself from the man's grasp, I somehow understood that the woman was deaf, which explained the volume of her sobs. After what seemed an hour of beating, the man ran off, leaving the woman on the ground, bloodied. Only then did the young man release me. At the same time, an old man with a long beard approached. He said the man was the woman's husband and that indeed the woman was deaf. Apparently, the woman wasn't able to collect trash because she had a leg wound, in which gangrene had set. Unable to rely on his wife for work, the husband had forced his five- and eight-year-old children to pick up the slack and sort trash in the city's dumps.

As Pooja continued to hug the little girl sitting in the dirt, I noticed her deformed hand, one finger hanging like a thread about to come loose. The materials with which Bombay's shacks are built, like asbestos and its derivatives, cause severe malformations in fetuses, which is why many children are born with physical disabilities. Pooja took the girl's other hand, lifted her up, and approached me.

"This is Lakshmi," she said, smiling again. "She is my best friend. She works now picking up trash because her mother's leg is bad and she can't work. Her younger brother will now also start working so they can buy food."

Pooja's mother signaled for me, which I obeyed immediately. Pooja took my left hand and Lakshmi grabbed me around the waist and forced a smile while she dried her tears. I approached the group of women who were all talking at the same time at the top of their lungs. I gathered that they were all trying to explain the battered woman's story. They had cleaned her face but couldn't stop her crying.

They kept pointing at the woman's leg, which was covered with a pretty purple sari. I bent down and lifted the sari as respectfully as I could. There were several flies in a wound that extended from her calf up to her thigh. The sight was as intolerable as the stench, especially because of the physical pain she was in—not only because of the wound and the beating, but also because of the intense moral pain; her family was having difficulty getting enough to eat because she couldn't work.

The women covered their noses with their saris while trying to hide their disgust. I wondered if they saw the same expression on my face, so I forced a smile, trying to see only the beautiful soul of that good woman.

The women continued to speak among themselves very loudly, and some of the men began participating in the conversation as well. The children played with a dead rat, and one of them was defecating as he put into his mouth some waste he had picked up from the ground. I was having difficulty swallowing and felt a great pressure in my chest. I felt insulted, offended, deceived by a world in which motorcyclists and Spanish women were all-important. How is it that I missed all of this, the squalor and pain, the humiliation and suffering? Had I been shown such scenes but just didn't see? What should I do now, I asked myself? Should I join the innocent and ignorant smiles of those children or the despairing cries of their mothers?

I was inside a nightmare in which faces appeared close up and then far away, distorted within a cloudy vision, surrounded by voices at once loud and soft, pleading and exhorting, filtered through a faulty microphone. I broke out in a cold sweat. I froze and hoped that something would happen to release me.

I COULDN'T EAT that night or the next morning, or for the next two days. Yet it wasn't the lingering vision of that festering leg and the anguish it caused that made me sick. It was the injustice of it all. I was internalizing what I couldn't accept in the twenty-first century and which, without an apparent reason, I felt responsible for. The nausea likely resulted from my unconscious reaction to, and rejection of, certain ideas that didn't belong to me, ideas and states of being in the world that I was not responsible for and that I had rejected. Yet my soul wouldn't release them or me.

Where were those smiles? Where were those poor children, so happy despite their state? Where was the warm and hospitable land? Where was the equilibrium within the desperate cries of that woman? And meditation? Transcendence? Where were such things to be found now?

I realized that those children were joyful but not happy. It is sensible to be joyful in life, but happiness is only possible if you have the freedom to choose. And they didn't. I imagined my parents, my grandmother, my friends in that situation, and sorrow fell on me like a brick, crushing my soul on that putrid floor. I began to see every person as an extension of myself, which is what they are, not in essence but in reality. Conversely, we are extensions of everyone else, all part of the harmonious universe.

I knew then that only if I saw and approached each individual as my own child, my own father, my own brother, as myself, could I hear in each voice and see in each sight the intense call for love that every person exudes.

FOUR

KAVITA

You should know that even as you gaze at a tree
and say to yourself that it is an oak or a banana tree,
those words, being part of botanical knowledge, have
conditioned your mind in such a way that it will insert
itself between you and the tree. To be in contact with
the tree we have to lay a hand on it. The word will not
help you touch it. —KRISHNAMURTI

The cabby drove through Marina Drive more slowly than usual for a Bombay taxi driver. Behind us, the Malabar hills stood high above the Arabian Sea, proudly displaying their opulent buildings, which were inhabited by thousands of Parsis, the wealthiest residents of the city. The Parsis are among the most powerful ethnic-religious communities in Bombay, even though the number of adherents to their religion has sharply diminished in the last few years because of their strict exclusivist matrimonial policy.

They are the descendants of the Persian Zoroastrians who fled the Muslims more than thirteen centuries ago. They established themselves in Bombay in the seventeenth and eighteenth centuries, occupying the highest circles of city life. An estimated seventy thousand Parsis live there today, mostly in neighborhoods that surround temples and restrict access for people who don't practice their religion.

That morning I had set myself the task of learning more about Parsis, and so I decided to dedicate most of the day to visiting their neighborhoods. In spite of the beautiful images that I encountered on my field trip, I couldn't get my mind off of Pooja and her friends in the slums. Little by little, new feelings emerged from my subconscious, feelings at once local and distant.

Everything I saw and everyone I met now was inexorably linked to the previous afternoon: a gesture, a sight, a color . . . on the sidewalks. I saw Pooja's lively eyes in every child's wink, and in each stern face I felt the pain of that woman with the gangrenous leg. I couldn't concentrate on anything else, for my soul remained in the slums with Pooja and her family and friends.

Finally the cab driver announced that we were at the Towers of Silence, about which I was enormously curious. The Towers of Silence are pillars where the

Parsis, following the protocol of their funerary rites, leave their dead to be picked apart by ravens and vultures. This community considers fire, earth, and water sacred. Thus they neither burn nor bury their dead. Nor do they throw their loved ones into the waters so that they can pass from this world to a better one.

There is no shortage of controversy surrounding the Towers of Silence. Because the vulture population of the city has declined, corpses are sometimes exposed for several days before they are shred to pieces by the birds. There, in the open, the bodies decompose, to the consternation of neighbors. Neither solar reflectors nor the chemical methods that Parsi communities have begun using have addressed the intense odors.

"I came to see the Towers of Silence. I am Spanish," I said innocently to the guards, while expressing surprise at the gates, because they seemed to promise a beautiful palace garden behind them. The guards explained that only Parsis were permitted to enter. I was disappointed but quickly understood that my first duty was to respect the community's privacy. And it now seemed horrendous to have been attracted by pillars with decomposing bodies.

At the end of the day I returned to Colaba, yet my thoughts remained in Dharavi. My mind traveled to the other side of the city, to the slums, those gray and brown oceans of misery that constitute a sad testament to privilege's ignorant conformity and poverty's opaque future. I began to question the Indians I met on the street, in restaurants, in museums. I educated myself about the condition of the millions of families living in the city's slums. Impassivity and ignorance wasn't an option any longer. The more I learned, the more horrified I became —for example, that families must pay "rent" to an extortion ring, even for a shack.

On the ride back to my hotel I read an interesting article by Mukesh Mehta about slum neighborhoods. Mehta is president of an important Indian advisory firm and the author of a well-known and controversial plan that proposes a viable alternative for constructing dignified dwellings in the slum area of Dharavi. Mehta included notes and numbers confirming the misery that others had mentioned to me, but which I had considered exaggerations. I had perhaps been consoling myself with the thought that reality had been distorted, made to appear crueler than it actually was.

THE SLUMS OF Bombay embrace—if that verb can be used in such a context—1.2 million families, with a population of more than 7 million people inhabiting 8,600 acres. The median income (understanding that in Bombay each family consists of at least seven people) is 40 dollars a month. The number of people living in the slums has increased dramatically in the last few years, mostly because of the arrival of families from rural India seeking to better their lives.

The Slum Improvement Program (SIP) was created in 1976—curiously, the year I was born—to provide community bathrooms and other facilities. That program has gone far in stanching the flow of misery but it hasn't cured the wound. In the middle of the 1990s, the government of Maharasthra instituted the Slum Rehabilitation Authority (SRA). The local press has been less than optimistic about the SRA's ethic and reliability. In brief, the government grants contracts to construction companies through the SRA, which designates inhabited land for building projects. In exchange, the construction companies must set aside some buildings for displaced families. It was soon discovered, however, that illegitimate payments were being made to SRA personnel in exchange for contractual wording favorable to the construction companies. At the end of the day, it seems, there is very little public housing favorable to families in the slums.

EVEN WHEN I VISITED tourist sites, my thoughts returned to Dharavi, Matunga, and Dadar. When I wasn't thinking about the slums, I thought about the dust in the city (and Bombay was the *best* city in India for someone with asthma) and imagined the diverse forms of asbestos boxes inhabited by more than half of Bombay's population.

Only a few days remained before I was to return to Spain, and I had no idea whether these thoughts of deprivation would fit in my luggage, much less in my life back in Barcelona. I doubted everything about my previous existence and was intensely and peculiarly sad about leaving India. I told myself that nearly everyone is sad to have to go home after vacation, that everyone regrets having to go back to work, to their everyday lives, perhaps to life itself.

Of course traveling allows us to consider the pigments of our daily lives back home, to see the colors more clearly. It is akin to watching a horror movie, where one is surprised that the character in the movie cannot sense the monster standing right behind him. We are that character. We don't notice our daily lives because we're inhabiting life, we're playing a role, we are inside our situation. Perhaps we should all learn to see our lives as movies, to reflect on our lives as if we were watching them on a movie screen. Would we see more clearly? Would we make wiser decisions? I don't know, but often the opposite is untenable.

During those last days in Bombay, I desperately sought someone to take me to the slums, to the farthest, most remote areas of Bombay. Finally, Ajay, who worked at the guesthouse where I was staying, took me to Borivali, in the north of the city.

"Stop here," I said impulsively after a few minutes crossing the slums in his Maruti Omni van. Once again I couldn't explain my sudden action. I seemed to be led by some inexorable force that guided me through passages flanked by cardboard and plastic. Soon we were followed by many children, some almost naked, others dressed in rags. They all had scabies marks on their thin arms.

I saw a shack at the end of the narrow street that was somehow different from the others. It was made out of blue plastic and was surrounded by garbage that, judging from the quantity, had been accumulating for a long time. Just outside, dressed in an impeccable white sari with silver borders, in contrast to her stark surroundings, was a young woman sobbing.

"Kavita, Kavita . . ." she repeated, compulsively rocking back and forth. On the ground in front of her, amid the garbage, lay a baby, about a month old, minuscule, motionless. For a moment I thought it might be one of those wrinkled plastic dolls designed to look like a newborn baby, pink skin and all. This baby was iridescent, sometimes brown, and sometimes almost purple.

"Kavita, Kavita . . ." the woman continued moaning. She looked at me bitterly and pointed toward the baby. Surprisingly, we were now surrounded by many people, and I sought in their gazes answers to the questions forming in my mind. And then I instinctively took the baby in my arms, a baby girl. She was dead.

"Her father drowned her," said Ajay behind me, startled. "If Kavita had lived, the family would have had to pay for a dowry." I was appalled, observing the faces around me, casually looking on. Gandhi said that if loving makes us hate others, it is better not to love. Nevertheless, at that moment, I hated profoundly. I hated the father who had drowned his own daughter, Kavita, and the hopes of his young wife. I hated the entire scene. I hated the man who had beaten his wife a breath short of death. I hated that Pooja had to live among such deprivation. I hated the world. I hated my impotence. I hated those people who stared at me, yet who seemed to look on innocently. I hated their innocence.

Kavita

I laid Kavita's body down. I instinctively touched her mother's feet to show my respect, as Hindus do. If reincarnation existed, Kavita was now a bird flying high in the sky, a free bird, I thought; or a pretty purple butterfly, the same color as the enigmatic sky that witnessed that scene with its crepuscular silence, perhaps with the same impotence I was feeling at the moment.

FIVE

NOOR

Does my changing have any significance whatsoever? . . .
This question is not correct, because you are the rest of
humanity. —KRISHNAMURTI

The Haji Ali mosque seemed to me one of the most
beautiful places in Bombay. This Muslim temple was built at the beginning of the eighteenth century and contains the tomb of the Sufi holy man Hazrat
Haji Ali. It is said that Haji Ali was a very wealthy mer-
chant who, after a visit to Mecca, abandoned material-
ism in favor of meditation. The temple's minarets stand
out from the surrounding sea and are especially beautiful when the light is dim, as when the sun sets and the
first lights come on.

Despite the building's splendor, the stone passage
over the sea that one must cross to get to the mosque
is not in the least enjoyable. Maimed beggars ask for

Allah's clemency and one's money. One such individual was a lively girl sitting on the ground intently observing me. She wore a burgundy dress edged with lace that must have once been white. She reminded me of Pooja. This girl, however, was older; her complexion revealed more maturity and her eyes less innocence.

"What is your name?" I asked her.

"Noor," she said with a clear voice.

"Noor. What a beautiful name! It means light, doesn't it?"

"Yes," she answered coquettishly, knowing her name was precious.

"How old are you?"

"I am ten."

"And you don't go to school?" I asked stupidly, knowing the answer.

"No, my mother works here, and I am with her. We beg tourists for money."

"Would you like to go to school?"

"Yes, but I can't. I am here and I help my mother. I can't go to school. She teaches me." She looked at the horizon.

"Noor, do you like ice cream?"

She quickly turned her head toward me, nodding from left to right in the purist of Indian styles. Her expression became childish and happy, and her black and penetrating eyes mirrored her disposition when she heard the magic words, "ice cream."

"Come on, Noor, let's buy a couple of ice creams in that store over there." At that moment, still smiling, she lifted her skirt and revealed two stumps. Her legs had been amputated below the thighs so that she could beg more effectively. Such occurrences are common in India, practiced on the smallest children, the most defenseless.

I went to get the ice cream, drying my tears as best I could, and we spent the afternoon together, surrounded by the Arabian Sea. Every stage has its lights and every street its lamps. Noor, with the light of her name and her eyes, lit the path on which I was walking, but the way was still obscure. One would have to be an insensitive beast not to be affected by the abhorrent scenes of Bombay, by Noor's condition. Yet it's easy to be sensitive and still not act. It's easy to act and still be a beast for selfish reasons. The question I asked myself, the question I increasingly became preoccupied with those last days in Bombay, was: Could I do something about so much misery? Did a solution exist inside of me? And if it did, was I capable, was I prepared, to do something about it?

AT TIMES I SEEMED on a precipice, other times on a plateau stretching beyond visibility. Sometimes an answer, a hint, seemed just within sight, almost within my reach. Other times not only this life but also the next life seemed futile. Certain scenes in India reinforced that futility.

For example, because only a few days remained before I was to return to Barcelona, I wanted to go to a place that I had read about in many articles and seen in documentaries. "Take me to Kamathipura," I said to the taxi driver. He braked hard, causing a screech louder than the decibels of Bombay's poor.

"I don't go there. You go if you want to, but not in my taxi," the driver pronounced emphatically. I got out of the car unperturbed. I would go on an elephant if necessary. I was determined and would not rest without having seen the neighborhood of Kamathipura. I took a train to Grant Road, and once there I intentionally got lost. I walked through different areas, some more brightly illuminated than others, some very busy, and others barely inhabited, in one case, just a sickly old man sleeping on a cardboard bed.

After wandering for two hours, I finally arrived at the red-light district of Kamathipura. The street was dark, flanked of course by red lights. I had paid little attention to warnings about this area. Any sense of danger was drowned by my curiosity and that inexorable force which still remained undefined. Kamathipura is considered the largest prostitution district in Asia; many wrongly attribute that dubious honor to Thailand. Many prostitutes working in Bombay's inner city are between seven and eighteen years old, sold by their families or kidnapped and transported from a neighboring country, like Bangladesh or Nepal. Such imports are known throughout the world.

The British created this zone in the nineteenth century as a "resting area" for troops. Kamathipura is the location for Andrew Levine's documentary, *The Day My God Died*, which I had seen some months before in Barcelona and which had impressed me greatly for journalistic precision, extreme cinematographic quality, and for the severity of the reality it exposes. I also remembered Kamathipura as the place where Maiti Nepal, the organization I had visited the year before on my trip to Kathmandu, rescued girls who had been kidnapped or sold by their families.

Hundreds of girls stood in front of the narrow doors of small clay houses ranging from one to three stories high, windows covered with shredded curtains. I tried to guess which street belonged to the girls, which to the boys, which to the transsexuals. Apparently, each area within Kamathipura has its market and its clients. I had been told that many prostitutes would offer their own children for a small additional sum.

The faces of some of the men there, probably the pimps, were anything but friendly. The danger was palpable. I knew someone was following me, yet I wasn't afraid because I had largely vanquished that word from my vocabulary.

Once again I impulsively looked into a doorway covered by half-opened curtains and walked in. The interior was dark, with a single red light on the stairs leading to the upper floor. I didn't think twice. I opened the curtains and walked up the stairs. If worse came to worst and someone stopped me, I could always say I was looking for a specific girl, or some such excuse.

The uneven, worn wooden stairs that creaked for mercy—located in a hallway not more than two and a half feet wide—announced my presence by the third step. On the second floor was another colored light illuminating a lone door covered by peacock-patterned curtains. I could hear a man groaning with pleasure, probably at the expense of a child. Instead of turning back, I drew the curtains aside.

The room inside was large enough only for the twin bed. The four walls were covered with photos of naked women. On my left, behind a small door, was another small room, covered by the same patterned curtain. I stood there taking in the posters and the humidity on the walls, visible even in the poor light, trying to ignore the moans. My concentration was broken by a boy who couldn't have been more than two years old, squatting there with an astonished look, his eyes like two oranges. He was putting something in his mouth. I smiled at him. He didn't move but slowly opened his mouth. Inside was what looked like a used condom. I tried to back up but bumped a pot on the floor. The moans in the adjacent room stopped, and the curtains parted.

"Priyanka?" A woman's voice. I turned and ran down the stairs without looking back, while I heard the voice of the young woman growing faint: "Priyanka? Priyanka?"

Back on the street I lost myself in the multitudes, desperately searching for an exit from the district. "Hell on earth." That's how an English journalist described Kamathipura. Stopping finally to catch my breath and calm down with the help of my inhaler, I remembered a phrase I had heard in Barcelona during one of my Raja yoga sessions: "Turn your heart into light; it is the only way that a dagger will not lance it when it strikes. If you make a mark on a stone, it will always be there; if you make it in a ball of light, the knife will go through it without leaving a trace."

I knew that I must do my best to erase that scene from my memory and, as a result, from my heart. I knew it would require enormous effort. I knew that if I succumbed to a sense of futility, if I threw up my hands at such scenes, the world and the people in it would be lost to me.

The days that followed were filled with car horns and children's smiles, pollution and beautiful land-scapes. My mind, my soul, and my heart remained in the slums, in Kamathipura, in Pooja's frightened eyes, in Kavita's lifeless body, and in the severed legs of Noor. I began planning my last day in the city while walking through Colaba. I would stroll around and buy souvenirs for my family. I would eat at Leopold's and would return to my hotel to watch the sunset in Chowpatty while eating a delicious *bhelpuri*.

As I was returning to my hotel, near Henry Road, I once again observed the children begging on the street corners, filthy, with lice-infested hair and God knows what else. I was overcome with sadness but felt no need to act. Even today I ponder my inability to act at that point despite my need to do so. As I said earlier, it still wasn't my time.

THE MORE I READ during those days—material devoured in taxis and rickshaws—the more I became alarmed about global poverty. More than a billion people live on less than a dollar a day; more than three billion have less than two dollars. Two billion people do not have access to medical assistance, and every day twenty thousand people die because of their poverty. Two-thirds of the population living in extreme misery are under fifteen years old, and 70 percent are women and children.

What is the difference between the developed and the lesser-developed world when 866 million people are illiterate, two billion do not have electricity, and 80 percent of the world's inhabitants don't have access to even the most basic of telecommunications? As an example of the so-called "equitable sharing" of resources on this planet, one need only consider that there are more telephone lines in Manhattan than in all of sub-Saharan Africa.

Khrishnamurti once wrote:

To see, to listen, is a great art . . . When we see, when we listen, we learn infinitely more than when we read books. Books are necessary, but to observe and listen sharpens one's senses.

I knew I still needed to see, to listen. Pooja and Priyanka had much more to teach me than all those books. That evening I didn't return to my hotel. Overcome by an indescribable feeling, I entered an Internet café. I looked up information about orphanages in Bombay. It is my duty to be interested, I thought. Perhaps I can visit one of those institutions and write an article that could be published in Barcelona and help to open the world's eyes. At least I am making an effort, I said to myself foolishly. I got in touch with Vinay Somani, head of Karmayog, a local networking service and arranged to meet him at his office near Flora Fountain.

"You only have a day left in Bombay?" he asked with an expression that inspired confidence. "It is very tight. Distances here are big, as you must know already. I don't know if you will be able to visit any orphanage. Many are on the outskirts of the city. I don't know."

"Please," I responded, "I insist. I would very much like to visit an orphanage or institution. I beg you, Mr. Somani, please help me." I rose from the comfortable chair. When he met my gaze with silence, I prepared to leave.

"Wait. There is one place where you could maybe go," he declared, and picked up the telephone.

"Atul? How are you? . . . Yes . . . Sure . . . Yes, of course . . . Yes . . . I know . . . Look . . . I have here a Spanish man, he is a journalist. Tomorrow is his last day in Bombay and in India, and he is asking me to visit an orphanage. He might be able to write something. Can I send him tomorrow? It will not be much time. He has to go at the end of the day . . . Yes? With you? Yes? Great! Perfect. I will tell him."

Vinay Somani hung up the phone and looked at me with a paternal smile. The orphanage was very small, on the outskirts of town. It housed forty kids and was having difficulty surviving because of lack of money.

Unable to hide my joy, I asked with curiosity, "What is the orphanage's name?"

"Kartika's Home"

"What a lovely name, Kartika's Home."

At last I would see an orphanage. Perhaps when I returned to Barcelona I would be able to help from there, although I suspected that everyday life might undercut my interest in the miserable reality that I had been experiencing the past few days.

SIX

KARTIKA'S HOME

"Where have I come from, where did you pick me up?"
the baby asked its mother.
    She answered half crying, half laughing, and clasping
the baby to her breast,—"You were hidden in my heart
as its desire, my darling." —RABINDRANATH TAGORE

I arrived early at the Gateway of India, so I strolled
around that tourist epicenter. The sun was warm and
comforted my skin. Soon, Atul Sharma, the man in
charge of Kartika's Home, appeared. Sturdy and seemingly good-natured, he looked at me pleasantly.

"Are you Jaume?" he asked.

"Yes, that's me."

We got into his car after small talk about Bombay
and my work as a journalist. His driver, William, was
a young man with a bushy moustache and very dark
skin. We traversed the city from north to south: Worli,
Mahim, Bandra, Santa Cruz . . . It seemed a goodbye to

Bombay, this last tour. My backpack was in the trunk, and later that night I would fly back to Barcelona, possibly never to see Bombay again.

The car windows were open, and I closed my eyes to the wind, trying to divine the future in the smells of past and present: the bitter stench of Pooja's neighborhood; the sea in which Noor couldn't stand; the fragrance, still fresh and sweet, of Kavita's lifeless body.

We crossed Andheri on a dusty road flanked by plastic tents where families, at that hour of the morning, were washing for the day.

"They rent children here," said Atul. I thought he had fallen asleep.

"I don't understand."

"Their parents or family rent them to beggars. If you beg with a child, you make more money. They line them up early in the morning to be rented for about twenty rupees a day. The beggars know they will be able to get more money from the people stuck in traffic. The children don't recognize the beggars that rent them, and they start crying. The younger they are, and the more they cry, the greater the profit for the beggar and therefore for the family . . ."

I tried to hide my shock, while also trying to understand what I had just heard. Soon the scenery changed.

Kartika's Home

In the northern parts of the city, the gray cement buildings gave way to mountains which, despite the dry season (it was still some months until the monsoons), were covered in lovely green shades: lime, bottle, olive . . . everything was beautiful. It reminded me of the Pyrenees, of the gorgeous landscapes of Catalonia's mountains, which I had seen so many times in my childhood. Among those peaks, some miles ahead, was the village of Vasai, in the center of which stood Kartika's Home orphanage.

"What a beautiful landscape, but what a long way off!" I exclaimed.

Atul started telling me about mountain places near the city. He didn't stop talking. Then suddenly I was overcome by a striking but enjoyable sensation: I could no longer hear what he was saying; I could only see his mouth moving. It was like an enormous light was shining on me—or maybe it was coming from me. It was as if, for a moment, I was listening to the most beautiful music I had ever heard, and it drowned out all other sensations.

"We have just entered Vasai territory. Kartika's Home is here," I heard Atul say as my reverie ended. Memory is nearly always distorted by consciousness. Yet I vividly remember that sensation. Some might call it a mystical experience, others a hallucination caused by exhaustion. All

I can say is that the sensation coincided exactly with our arrival in Vasai.

We entered a dusty street, full of trucks. You could still see the mountains above the garages and warehouses. A few minutes later, we turned into a development. On one side of the main entrance, which was about fifteen feet wide, was a rusty welcoming sign: WESTERN PARK COMPLEX, LUXURY BUNGALOWS. On the other side was a security post.

"Welcome to Kartika's Home," Atul said.

"Is this Kartika's Home? The orphanage? But this is a housing development . . ."

"We have rented a small house here—that's where the children live. It's a quiet place, a run-of-the-mill development."

The idea pleased me. Children weren't interned or shut away, like those I had seen at orphanages so many times before. Here was a home. "Normality," I wrote in my tiny notebook. Yet the orphanage was somehow rundown. The sign outside, a small square of wood, was twisted and tied to a railing with a worn-out cordon: KARTIKA'S HOME ORPHANAGE, REGISTERED ORGANIZATION.

When I crossed the small patio and entered the house, it was love at first sight, as they say. The children stared at me in amazement. Someone must have told them to expect a visitor that day. They seemed to have been waiting their entire lives. I'm certain that I was the first white person some of them had ever seen.

"Please be seated. There is no reason to keep standing," said Atul. Forty boys and girls sat on the ground in unison without batting an eyelash.

"Good morning."

"Good morning, uncle," they answered with timid yet curious voices.

We played *carrom*, a game played with counters on a board that has holes in its corners; we talked, we laughed. They asked me about Spain. On the wall was an old map, and I asked them to locate my country. They pointed to the United States. I've since learned that geography isn't among many Indians' strengths.

"Uh, oh . . . your geography is not very good!" I told them jokingly.

They laughed, instinctively covering their mouths with their hands.

"Don't cover yourselves! Look what pretty smiles you have," I said, and they answered with even more smiles. Gaining confidence, the smallest children began playing and jumping on my back. The oldest asked me thousands of questions, observing and nodding, intently acknowledging each answer. I thought about Pooja,

Noor, and the rascals I had met in Bombay's streets during the trip, and I understood that the children I saw before me now had come from similar or worse conditions. They were all prisoners of a society that had condemned them to the jail of poverty and injustice, angels of a forgotten heaven.

"Which school do they attend?" I asked Atul, who seemed to have had enough of my incessant questioning.

"We give them some instruction here, in the garage. We cannot afford to send them to a private school. We would like to, but we can't. And the public school in this district is always closed. It is a small shack for all the millions of kids of the district."

They told me about some individual cases and the previous lives of the children. I asked them to please talk quietly and discreetly, so as not to hurt anyone's feelings. On the steps leading up to the second floor sat a girl observing the scene with a smile. She was wearing a *kurta pajama*.

"Who is she?"

"Her name is Goopta. Her father used to rape her," Atul answered in a whisper.

"What an atrocity!"

"Not only her father, but also her two grandfathers, paternal and maternal, and her two brothers."

I was silent.

"Her mother, to save her from that situation . . . brought her here?" I finally asked.

"No. She sold her to a brothel in Kamathipura. We got her from there."

"And that girl with a green shirt?"

"Her name is Archana. She was sold into prostitution at five years old. The vaginal tears were indescribable."

"And that older boy over there?"

"His name is Raj. We found him in Churchgate Station. We don't know who his father is. His mother is an alcoholic. When he was a baby, she used to cut his arms with a knife. One night, when he was six years old, he escaped. He went to live at Churchgate Station. He began hanging out with street gangs, inhaling glue, and stealing wallets."

I noticed a smiling boy with bangs cut in the shape of a bowl. "What about that boy over there? Who is he?"

"His name is Rohit. His grandfather brought him yesterday. His parents died, and the grandfather says he is much too old to take care of him. He wanted to ensure his grandson's future with a roof to sleep under."

"He looks happy."

"Well . . ."

"What's the matter?" I asked, surprised.

"He is epileptic. He has suffered several serious episodes in the last few months. We don't know what to do."

"Can't you take him to the doctor? There must be a treatment!"

"Yes, but it costs five hundred rupees a month, and we don't have the money. We are in a very precarious economic situation." Five hundred rupees was about thirteen dollars.

"And what happens if you cannot pay for the treatment in the next few months?"

With sincere sadness, Atul lowered his gaze and said nothing.

"We are in the red; we can hardly pay for the children's food. But please, do not write that in your article. Say that we need help, but do not explain the situation."

Outside, two men observing the place from a car caught my attention. They stared me down.

"Who are they?"

"We don't really know. They have been prowling around for days. We think they might be pimps from a Kamathipura brothel. They are waiting for the orphanage to close, to select children to work for them."

"Can that really happen?" I asked, stunned. It was like being inside a thriller with a bad ending.

"Yes, it could happen," said Atul. "Please, write an article so that someone helps us."

I understood then, very clearly, what is meant by a "broken heart." I felt an oppressive weight within my chest, as if my heart were being torn apart. The shreds kept falling off all the way back to the airport. If ever I decide to return to this place, I thought, amid my tears, I need only follow that trail of shreds.

WHEN I ARRIVED at Bombay's Chhatrapati Shivaji International Airport, I boarded my flight with the pain of memory, with the painful knowledge that I was leaving those children behind. Sitting next to me, an Indian nun tried to smooth out the wrinkles in her habit while getting comfortable. She asked me if I was a member of a religious order.

"I, a brother?" I responded.

I studied my reflection in the airplane's window. What had compelled this good woman to think I was a member of some kind of religious group?

The flight was a struggle. A million thoughts raced through my head while I gazed at the darkness outside. Every so often I turned to take in the kind face of that nun, who always returned my gaze with a smile. It was as if she were telling me that I wasn't wrong, that the crazy ideas beginning to form in my mind weren't so crazy, that they carried the mark of my soul.

I tried to relax by reading Tagore:

What does it matter if we fail to derive the exact meaning of this great harmony? Is it not like the hand meeting the string and drawing out at once all its tones at the touch? It is the language of beauty, the caress, that comes from the heart of the world and straightway reaches our heart.

Reading this passage, I remembered a phrase from my grandmother Martha: "Do it if your heart tells you so." My heart was telling me many things, all difficult to understand. But the force with which it was speaking was unmistakable.

SEVEN

THE WHITE WALL

Endure, even if alone and everyone is against you.
Look them in the eyes, even if they are calling for
blood. Do not be afraid. Trust the heart's voice that
asks you to abandon everything and everyone. You
must be prepared to die for that which gives your
life meaning. —GANDHI

The first thing I did after I returned to Barcelona was
to meet with two NGOs. I explained the orphanage's situation and asked them for help. This was much
more complicated than I had anticipated. Some organizations said it was outside their geographical scope;
others asked me to submit a proposal for the following
year's campaign; others simply wished me luck.

I was troubled by this lack of enthusiasm, the un-
willingness to help children in need. I had known be-
forehand that the task wouldn't be easy, but I wasn't
prepared for such negativity. The children's situation at

the orphanage was becoming increasingly dire as the days passed. I had to act fast.

There are places in life that seep into your soul, becoming forever a part of it. You need encounter such places only once for your life to be unsuspectingly, and perhaps subtly, altered. Profound conversations and transcendental decisions are found in such places, moments forever inhabiting the deepest corners of memory: a bench in a remote park, a dark street corner, a small plaza, a doorstep. They are there, these places, in the soul, to be called up when one's ability to carry on, to persevere, is tested.

Here was my test: to help this orphanage, which somehow wasn't a priority for many others. One by one, I visited the places in Barcelona that meant the most to me—those corners where tears had been shed, where smiles had been fed. What, exactly, was I looking for? Invisible words, full of unalterable memories? Silent accomplices? Whispers working on my behalf with respect to the right path?

I took long walks. I meditated and thought about what I should do to save those kids from an unpromising future. If you walk past a house on fire and a child inside is crying for help, what would you do? Would you look for a telephone to call the fire department? Or would you react instinctively, rushing inside that burning house to save the child whose cries seem directed at you? Most of us know the answer.

If no one else is willing to help save those children from the flames of poverty and misfortune, I thought, I will save them myself. I will look for the resources and do everything necessary to ensure that those kids don't return to the brothels of Bombay. I will make it—them—my life, for the rest of my life.

Despite the clearing in the distance, I was filled with doubt. Why these children? Why now? There have always been poor and needy people in the world. Indeed, there have always been such people in my own city.

Destiny is at play here, I thought. Perhaps the same destiny that brings two lovers together from opposite sides of the world. Why does a man from Madrid, for example, leave family and friends, give up possessions, to live with his beloved in Australia, or in Canada? Destiny doesn't answer such questions, it only prompts them. Some call this destiny "God," others "fate"; still others, "chance." Common to all is their scope: they are beyond understanding.

And so I embarked on what many considered a crazy endeavor. I immediately recognized I would have to give up almost everything to provide for the orphanage. I called Atul to find out how much money the orphanage owed. My own income wasn't much more than what any young journalist might earn. I did the math. The bottom line wasn't convincing, yet it was a buried treasure for those children in Bombay.

The first person I told about my decision was my father, the next, my maternal grandmother, Marta. (My grandmother had always lived in my parents' house, and when my mother had died eight years earlier she stayed with us.) Discreet, wise, and patient, my father is one of those people who advise others to count to ten before making important decisions. I knew he wouldn't approve of the project, although he would not forbid it. I anticipated his thoughts, imagining that he would blame my decision on alienation produced by the emotional shock of my trip.

"Dad," I said, "you know I visited an orphanage during this last trip. It's called Kartika's Home. There are forty kids there, the most fantastic and loving children I have ever met. The orphanage is going through a rough period. I've tried in the last few days to find help, but haven't had any luck. I know you'll think I'm crazy, but I assure you, I'm convinced of the direction I must take. And I'm certain of my decision: I'm going to take charge of the orphanage."

"But how will you do it?" he asked. "With what money? You're not exactly doing great financially. Do you know how many expenses an orphanage might have?"

"The first thing I'm going to do is to get rid of everything I have that might be worth something. I'll sell it and will have a little something to begin."

"You won't have enough even for the start, my son, really."

"Then I'll make the most of any help I can find. I'll contact the people I've met at work in the past. What's the use of all those contacts otherwise? And I'll work on finding new contacts. I'll create an umbrella organization so that funds go directly to the orphanage. Everything will be transparent."

"But, son, do you realize what this entails? It's an enormous job. Where will you find the time?"

"I'll need a lot of time. That's why I'm quitting both my jobs. I have some money saved. I'll be able to survive for a few months. And if you don't object, I'll live with you."

"Of course you can come here. This is your house, you know that. But please think about what you're saying and think it through. I wouldn't do it. Whatever you do, you know that I'll always respect your decision. But think it over, Jaume. Think it through carefully . . ."

He responded exactly as I had expected. Many times in my life, before making a decision, I've asked myself what my father would do, or not do. And if I wasn't prepared to accept the answer, I would think it over several times more before making a decision.

My father is one of those people who always find the middle ground. His advice and enduring patience are fountains of serenity. And of course there was my mother who, as a teacher, devoted her life to the education of children, including me. Her generous love was unequivocal. My parents never preached or scolded, but taught by example. And from their example, I learned about love, about the value of respect and affection. I profoundly believe that such an education is not only most effective but also most sensible.

My father didn't disappoint me. I told him of my intention to move to Bombay. I told him that Bombay was where I could really help, that it was necessary to live there, at least in the first months, to launch the project most effectively. I said I would return to Spain immediately if something happened at home—if, for example, he or my grandmother became sick.

The next day I met Sonia and Miguel Angelo for lunch at La Mamasita, on Sarriá Avenue, very near to where Sonia worked. She and I had worked together some years before and we had become good friends. Miguel Angelo had also become a good friend. We laughed that we only saw each other on Wednesdays or Thursdays, and so we always had to choose from the same "menu of the day."

I was impatient when they arrived because I had spent the morning at the government offices of Catalonia, where lawyers explained the steps required to create an entity. Of course bureaucracy would work against me, especially because there was no time to lose. I tried to pick the best moment to tell Sonia and Miguel of my plans. Their immediate support and enthusiasm filled me with hope, both of which I would need. They will never know how decisive their reaction was, and how important it was for me.

"You will need a website," Miguel Angelo said. "Think about a name and let me know. Maybe I can design it, and you won't have to pay for a designer." Thus we spent the rest of that wonderful meal advancing ideas and dispelling illusions. While we discussed the endeavor, I thought about my dream and tried to visualize it.

After completing the initial paperwork, I waited for what seemed an interminable amount of time, which was frustrating. Yet I knew it paled in comparison to what lay ahead for me in Bombay. And it's fair to say that everyone at the government office was helpful and efficient.

Meanwhile I sought support and advice. I had no team in Barcelona or in Bombay. Except for a few friends, like Miguel Angelo, I did everything myself. When I did seek help, my pleas were met with the same incredulousness as my solicitations for financial support:

"It is an outlandish idea. I don't believe it is at all possible. It's impossible for a young man like you, with an easy life, to stomach a country like India. They will eat you alive. You'll be completely out of it. I definitely won't help you. And believe me, I'm doing you a favor by not helping you. You will fry. I give you three months. Think about it. Let those who want to fix the world help, those who know what they're doing. Don't get mixed up."

Another replied that I should be spending my time chasing girls: "At your age you should be going into clubs, flirting, riding your motorcycle. You're young, a professional. You're going to work with an orphanage as if you're a monk? What about your life? What crazy girl will marry you? An Indian woman? Those people are peculiar and different . . . you're crazy . . ."

An alarmed colleague said I knew nothing about putting together and managing such a project. "Do you have any experience in international cooperation?" he asked.

They told me at work that I was throwing away a brilliant career. Not one of these arguments convinced me. I might be throwing away a brilliant journalistic future, I thought; I might not. What I knew with certainty was that the light of forty stars is much stronger than the light of one.

And then there were such absurd responses as: "Did you fall on your head?" "But you are so young and so handsome!" "Have you gone crazy?" "What tragedy has stricken you?" "Did your girlfriend leave you?" "Did they fire you?" "Aren't you happy?" "Are you going to India to find yourself?" "Are you involved with a sect? Be careful, it is very dangerous" . . . and so on.

Amid the uproar the wise writings of Gandhi filled my nights, and I took much comfort from his wisdom:

We must not let ourselves be taken away by the current. A human being cannot save others if he drowns.

I remember one such night. I had to register the organization's name the next day. They had told me at the government office that it might be possible to get a provisional document that would enable me to begin funneling funds to the orphanage once I had a registered name. I had a thousand ideas. I had a notebook and a pen. By morning, I thought, I would have that name.

I closed my eyes and began to think about the children. I wrote the first words that came to mind. I told myself that, since my heart led me into the venture in the first place, my heart must decide the name.

I took flight in the darkness, crossing half the world to the slums of Bombay. I flew over Italy and the Middle East. I saw the Jordanian ruins that I had visited during my first trip. I cried over the Arabian Sea, which I had stepped into just a month earlier. I took flight and I flew, finally arriving at Kartika's Home. I saw Pooja, Rohit, Shakuntala, Priyanka, Gopta . . . I saw them in the garages of the little houses, playing, laughing, singing, braiding their hair, putting on coconut oil for school.

And then it was clear! And (as so often happens when an idea becomes clear) I said to myself, Why didn't I think of that before? In sun or shadow, cold or heat, those children did not stop smiling. I jumped from my bed and sat up. I turned on the light, took my pen and wrote "Smiles."

I went back to bed, calm and satisfied, even though a single word wasn't enough. The lawyers had told me that the name had to reflect the organization's mission and, if possible, its geographical scope. I turned the lamp on again, and I added "Bombay Smiles."

Yes, I liked that name. So much so that, lying in darkness, I was showered with white sparkles from the other side of the world, filling me with the innocence of those children, with the purity of their souls, with the injustice and pain of their condition.

I was told the name would be registered and that I would receive a permit promptly.

The first person I shared the name with was Miguel Angelo. He loved it and said he would register the domain and begin designing the web site right away. Now we needed money. During the next few days, I knocked on every door imaginable, making call after call, from seven in the morning until midnight. Every second wasted increased the chance that those children in Bombay might end up in a brothel.

Several people offered support. Others laughed and said that helping children on the other side of the world wasn't their problem. "After all," more than one person said, "one or two people cannot save the world." Of course, I disagreed.

Some people offered to organize fundraising events —and to keep half the revenue. I left many meetings horrified. Luckily, others showed enormous heart.

"What can we do for you?"

"Nothing for me," I usually replied, "but I'm going to tell you about some children in Bombay for whom you can do a lot." Then I showed them the small photo album I carried around and which steeled my soul when I encountered stares or rejection. That album was my Duracell battery, my energy source.

I put my journalistic skills to work in those meetings, and only then did I feel that perhaps destiny might have influenced my decision to study journalism—for I am convinced that the true essence of an action or event has a gestation period. When that essence or "truth" emerges, it does so for the benefit of another person or group of people rather than for oneself.

I understood right then the purpose of my studies, why my dissertation was on Rwanda's genocide, and why I took that trip . . . I even saw destiny in the fact that my first interview as a journalist had been with Vicente Ferrer, about whom I barely knew anything at the time.*

One meeting led to another and, finally, to funds. While a journalist, I always respected interviewees' off-the-record comments. I published positive articles

*Vicente Ferrer was a well-known Catalan secular missionary who worked in India, where he established the organization *Rural Development Trust* in 1970.

about certain companies that were going through difficult times. These were some of the people that came through for me. They could hardly say no.

THEY SAY EVERYTHING you do in life comes back to you in some form or another. I agree.

It's always best to live honestly and straightforwardly, for the truth makes us happy. The calm and satisfaction that it brings cannot be bought. Period.

I recognized then the enormous degree of responsibility we have toward one another. We spend our lives criticizing and complaining about the world, saying it's going to hell, yet very often we forget that we are part of that world. We must change ourselves before we can change the world. It *all* begins in us, and everything is reducible to us.

It's as if we have before us a black wall. We do nothing but complain of the darkness, do nothing but fear the darkness. Yet right beside us sits a gallon of white paint and a paint brush. That gallon of paint might cover only a portion of the wall. But if each person paints his and her portion, or just a portion of a portion, the wall will eventually turn white.

EIGHT

THE REST OF MY LIFE

Truth resides in every human being's heart. It is there
when we need guidance. It is not important how it
reveals itself to us. We cannot impose our own vision of
reality on others. —GANDHI

Several weeks went by, and contributions for the orphanage were still lacking. My first priority was to
stop the hemorrhaging at the orphanage, which could
be done with small donations. Such donations would
also enable me to establish a more durable strategy.

I got a break when people helped me organize a
benefit concert featuring the singer Antonio Orozco.
The proceeds would fund one year of the children's education. Even the waiters worked for free that night.

"We are doing this because we love you," they said.

"It is not for me," I insisted, "but for the children in
Bombay."

My friends from the restaurant, Sonia and Miguel Angelo, with whom I first shared my thoughts about the orphanage, were the first contributors. They designed the organization's website, as promised. I also contacted the Parisian photographic studio of Olivier Föllmi, an established institution that has brought the world beautiful images of India, Nepal, and Tibet for years. Mr. Follmi had developed his own foundation for the most disadvantaged. He responded to my pleas with a wonderful letter, saying that he would let me use his images for my cause.

I flew to Bombay after a delirious month and a half, with enough hope and donations to carry the orphanage in the short term. The orphanage would not be closing. I would be staying at one of the teacher's homes until I could find modest lodgings. I did not want to stay at the orphanage. As in many places in the world, gossip flourishes in India. I didn't want to take any chances with respect to the children and what others might think about a foreigner's relationships with them. For the first time in a long time, I slept calmly; I was happy. It was done—those children were safe. Another piece had been fitted into the world's puzzle.

Thereafter I never thought about my life again. I only thought about others, specifically, the children at the orphanage. I now inhabited the secret of happiness: the happiness that accompanies our tending to other people's happiness. There are no words for such joy.

After receiving the necessary provisional permits in Barcelona, I recall spending my entire day hugging the documents to my chest. I didn't even put them down to eat lunch. The hopes of many children depended on those papers.

Several donations came through, and I established a program for increasing support and for housing more children at the orphanage. Still, I had to increase the project's exposure: I couldn't rely solely on friends and contacts. I met a businesswoman, the owner of several companies that had grown sizably over the past few years. "What can I do to get more funds? What system would you use? What should my strategies be?" I peppered her with questions. "Look Jaume," she answered, "just keep doing what you are doing right now with me. Keep talking about your project with the same passion. Rely on that passion when you're speaking in public. The words will come easily to you—everything will flow. If you retain your passion and let it show, the organization will be very successful."

Funding aside, we agreed that the family structure should be maintained at the orphanage. I established one condition: Should the orphanage grow, it must retain its original arrangement—one that might have emerged from economic necessity. I wanted to preserve the semblance of a family unit. As the orphanage grew, the residences should continue to be small houses, each with a married couple in charge of a handful of children.

When we think of an orphanage, we often imagine an enormous hall lined with bunk beds where love was long ago locked out, a place ruled by a strict warden who continually threatens the children. That was the last thing I wanted for those children. Of course, any proper education involves discipline. Living in small houses with married couples would enable the children to experience a home, while at the same time receiving support and affection as the main ingredients of their development. Love would motivate them to grow, to learn, to gain the self-confidence they would need to live independent lives.

A child can attend the best school and get the best education money can buy, can have the healthiest nutrition, can have access to the best doctors for mental and physical health. Yet a lack of love will obliterate these advantages. Love trumps all. Ideally, of course, one should have access to good schools, healthy food, etc., but everything begins with love. It is the most stable foundation.

How many times have we seen wealthy people who appear lost to the world because they didn't experience parental love as children, having been shuffled from nanny to nanny instead?

I learned three important lessons in those first few weeks. I had to exercise humility, humor, and patience —humility first. Gandhi wrote that there is much lying in our world because we all claim the "right to an illuminated conscience without discipline." He went on to say that in order to discover the truth, one must begin with a great sense of humility. To "enter into the heart of truth's ocean . . . it is necessary to become nothing."

It became clear on the first day at the orphanage that I was at the service of the children and not the other way around. I was their servant, their vassal: I had come to their land and renounced everything so that they could order me around, so that they could impose their needs on me. I learned to listen before acting. I learned not to assume anything, including that I was needed. Those children didn't need anything from me, from a Westerner. They could teach me much more than I could teach them.

"What is the meaning of your name?" they asked incessantly, pronouncing it differently each time the question was asked.

"Jaume comes from the Hebrew 'Jacob' and means 'God will reward.'"

"How pretty!" said some, while others repeated my words to the ones who hadn't heard.

I needed stamina, too. I was still a twenty-something-year-old kid. Yet one who had replaced the pleasures of riding his motorcycle around Barcelona and watching the girls in the square with preserving the futures of the children of Bombay. Dreariness wouldn't be permitted. The repercussions for my non-governmental organization—for the children—would be too great.

I recognized the importance of "keeping it together" after Atul first sent me the children's files, when I was still in Barcelona soliciting contributions. I began to cry while reading the documents in a Barcelona coffee shop: I wasn't reading some printed words on a worn-out piece of paper about "Third World children." I was reading about Pooja, Babu, and Neeta, and the other children I had met. I was able to put a name, face, and smile to each sentence in the stories. Such emotions were overwhelming.

Soon thereafter I built a small "recycling plant" within me. I decided I would recycle each instance of sorrow I witnessed in Bombay, converting that sorrow into energy that could go toward the orphanage. I recognized the weight now on my shoulders. I recognized that sentimental weakness could endanger the project. I couldn't be weak or soft. Perseverance and fortitude would carry the day. Perseverance and fortitude *had* to carry the day.

During the second week at the orphanage, when I had begun to feel comfortable and when the paperwork for foreign aid had been completed, it was decided that I would teach the children Spanish. It was a sunny April day and I was nervous. Our first Spanish class! There was a small garage on the side of the house where the older children lived; it was used as the school. The walls were cracked and weathered from the last few monsoons. The smell of mildew greeted us at the door. The wallpaper was beyond color.

I hovered outside the doorway, observing the children in the classroom, with their worn notebooks and their pencils used to the stub. I noticed that some were smiling and whispering; someone was writing on the blackboard around the corner.

"The teacher is silly." "This white man is a fool." I imagined numerous scenarios of shame. I was met with silence and shiny eyes when I finally entered the room. I turned toward the blackboard, ready to respond with an annoyed gesture to some phrase teasing "Jaume sir," as they called me. In English, in large, clear script were two sentences:

> *Jaume means God will reward.*
> *God has rewarded us with Jaume.*

I was overcome with emotion and asked for forgiveness from all the gods for having doubted their kindness.

THE NEXT DAY, while I was in my office studying Hindi, two orphanage workers came in, alarmed.

"Jaume ji, Jaume ji!" That was the first time that I heard my name with the attached suffix *ji*, a mark of the greatest respect in India, and it made me uncomfortable.

"What is it? Calm down please!"

"You have to go to Matunga please, it is very important. Something horrible has happened. We have to go there quickly, we have to go or it will be too late."

"Too late for what? I don't understand anything. Can you please explain?"

"Something has happened in the slums district, Jaume ji. A woman who had been attacked by her husband several times with acid crushed his brain with a big stone while he was sleeping. The four children were there. The police are going to arrest her. The children will be by themselves."

We drove as fast as we could, that is, as fast as the old van, potholes, and traffic would allow. When we arrived, I saw four children, two of them really young. They were crying incessantly and shaking. The three girls were less than ten years old, and the boy was around two. Their clothes were covered with something white, which I later learned was brain matter; it was all over the walls, too.

The police had left a while before. Someone in a nearby shack had told the police that he knew their maternal uncles and would contact them in their native Tamil Nadu. Yet my instinct told me that those children were unprotected. I turned and noticed the unwelcome presence of several men, the same men who had sat in the van outside the orphanage several months earlier, observing the children. I don't know what made me recognize them, but my memory is largely photographic. I knew instantly who they were.

One of them was on his phone while he stared at his shiny shoes. The other was chatting with the woman who, minutes earlier, assured everyone that she was the uncles' friend. The children were still crying, surrounded by many strangers. The two men looked alike, taller and stronger than the typical Indian. They were about forty years old and had thick moustaches. They wore perfectly ironed shirts and tight pleated pants. And their shoes, black leather slip-ons, were so shiny they seemed to be patent leather.

I addressed them, completely ignoring the advice of some people in the room.

"Is there a problem? If you agree . . . let's go together to the police station and decide there what to do with the children. And if you don't agree, we will go anyway." We argued and argued. Somehow I got the best of them. Finally they left, but not without revealing the hate they had for me: they spat on my feet. It was the first time that happened to me. It wouldn't be the last, nor would my feet be the only target.

I was enormously satisfied, not only with the outcome of the argument, but also with the effect of my words—how they had overcome violence. The woman who had said she was part of the family left quickly after the men, feigning not to know what was happening. I followed her. Or more precisely, I ran after her because she was now running. I had to know what the hell was on the paper she was clasping in her left hand, which she had shown to the thugs minutes earlier.

It is true that curiosity can kill a cat. It is also true that curiosity can serve a person well. I finally caught up with the woman and grabbed her arm. She dropped the paper and quickly disappeared between piles of garbage. I couldn't understand anything because the writing was in Hindi. I found someone to translate.

"It is the price for each of the children. They were trying to sell them."

After cleaning the children with a bucket full of water provided by a neighbor, I called the police to try to discover where the mother had been taken. Then I began to consider the children and their immediate future. I couldn't just take them. That would have been kidnapping. We had to get legal authorization and permission from the children's guardian, a very difficult procedure considering the father was dead and the mother in jail.

We had to find the children's papers and birth certificates. If they weren't in the shack, which was probable since the family was not from Bombay, or the children had not been registered—like many children—we would have to go to the government of the state in which they were born. At the same time, we would have to initiate another approval process with the central government in Delhi, in order for our organization's commissioner to approve an addition to the orphanage without demanding to profit from the procedure himself.

Also, since I—a white man—was involved, everything would be much more complicated. Three months later, we finally took those children in at the orphan-age. They gradually began opening up and trusting us. We needed to meet them on their terms, at their own rhythms.

A few days later, Jitesh and Robita, two of the guards at the orphanage, told me that a cousin of someone they knew needed our help. His name was Santosh; he was fourteen and his father had died a few weeks earlier. Apparently he lived near Dadar Station in an area used as a refuse dump. He had settled there with his father when they emigrated from Rajasthan following his mother's death. After his father's death, Santosh had begun hanging out with the station's street gangs, and his physical state was deteriorating.

When we got to Dadar, we could not find the gang, so we decided to explore another part of the station, one hidden from the thousands of passengers who take the train each day in that terminal. We saw a group of kids sniffing glue from transparent bags and laughing, shar-ing coarse jokes and speaking in words that they could hardly articulate.

"Which of you is Santosh?"

"That one there," said one of them, assuming a pro-vocative attitude typical of his status. Santosh was thin, very dark, and was lying down, his head resting on a wooden box. In his left hand he held a plastic bag, in his right, a joint. His eyes were vacant, and for a moment I wondered whether he was alive. Suddenly, he went into convulsions, and then, as we were holding him, he vomited a pink fluid.

We had to rush him to a hospital. The paperwork would have to wait. Before we left, I turned to look at the other kids, who continued sniffing and smoking. Who knows whether they are still alive? I thought about Babita, Ankita, Neeta, and Jitendra. How many children like them are sold into servitude or die because someone doesn't stop to help? And the same thing would have happened to Rati, Vinayak, Rameeta—and the others we took in afterward.

Soon I added one more premise to my "recycling plant": I would never take pride in my actions. I would always focus my mind on the problem at hand. I had been in India for a few months by that time, but already I was being overwhelmed by events, by children needing help. I felt as if I had been in the country for a year. I knew the names of the neighborhoods and could locate them on a map. And I now knew how to bargain with the best of hustlers. I had solved, in my mind, the urban and geographical references of the Bombay labyrinth.

"YOU SHOULD WORK LESS and have more leisure time," said some of the teachers at the orphanage. So one afternoon I accepted an invitation to stroll with them along Linking Road, a commercial street in Bombay's Bandra district. Shopping had never been a favorite activity. I wasn't enthusiastic about losing so much time. We entered a men's clothing stall, filled from top to bottom with tuxedos, plastic pearls, and golden turbans.

On one side were displayed a number of *Punjabi kurta* or *Punjabi pajama*, typical street wear. Most seemed ostentatious, but some were made of rough silks and damasks, and were handsome.

"Do you like them? They are pretty, aren't they?" asked Atul, compulsively checking the price tags.

"They are beautiful, yes, but look at the prices. It is impossible to buy one. Look at this one, three thousand rupees, that is . . . sixty dollars! I can't afford this, it's very expensive!" I told them the prices were equivalent to a month's rent for one of the houses. I knew my salary and theirs. And I knew none of us could afford it.

I remembered at that moment the decision I had made back in Barcelona—once I knew I was going to devote my life to the children of Bombay—to give away the suits and accessories sent to me during the three years I worked at the restaurant (I will keep that place in my heart forever), as well as the ties I wore as a journalist. I realized then that it isn't difficult to renounce material possessions. What one misses most is what one cannot buy. I did not need masks or costumes anymore. I needed only what was needed by the orphanage. No disguises were needed or tolerated there. A couple of shirts, two pairs of pants, a pair of sandals, and a pair of winter shoes would suffice.

As I mentioned earlier, more than a few people were concerned about me at the time I was renouncing my possessions and asking for money to help the children at the orphanage. They thought something bad had happened to bring about this life-changing decision. Of course someone in my position couldn't avoid latent dissatisfaction, nor could I eliminate such dissatisfaction. I had been happy, but I was not fleeing from "my life." The move I was making had to emerge from within, organically; it could not be bought nor rationalized.

"Tell us which one you like, and we will take a picture of you wearing it. Just put it on over your clothes, and we'll take the picture," they all said.

They seemed delighted with the bright idea, and their enthusiasm was infectious. I chose a handsome burgundy suit. The neckline had subtle beading, giving it a solemn air.

"You look like a maharaja" they exclaimed, clapping. In good spirit, they next insisted I try on a beige *dupatta* trimmed with the same color as the *Punjabi*. The shop assistant said that he could not sell the two pieces together, because the long shawl was part of another suit, but my colleagues insisted. A group of people had formed around us, and everyone was laughing. Finally the picture was taken and everyone was happy.

The next week we organized *carrom* tournaments for the children and handed out trophies. I also began to give journalism classes. I planned to develop a magazine with the older kids. We would call it the *Kartika Times*, and they could publish their own stories and interviews. Such activity would stimulate their creativity and bring them closer to one another, especially at the "editorial board" meetings. Everyone opened up splendidly.

One day after school, when I returned to my room, I was greeted by that burgundy *Punjabi kurta* with the beige *dupatta*. It was displayed on the wall above my bed. Next to it was a note:

> *Thank you very much for what you do for us.*
> *Kartika's Home teachers and personnel.*

The Rest of My Life

Everyone had pitched in to buy the suit. I'm sure it took much effort. Their gratitude was boundless. My gratitude was boundless, to them and to God.

I REMEMBER WANTING things to work out with respect to the formal papers and the funding before I returned to Bombay, even before I got in touch with Atul again. I didn't want to destroy his and the others' hopes. Once that had been achieved and I was able to tell Atul that the orphanage *would* be able to remain open, with aid, and that I would explain when I returned to Bombay, I recall clutching the phone to my heart. I gazed at a bedside photograph of one of the children. I had two days to pack my suitcases, which I filled mostly with items for the children. I wouldn't just be taking another trip to Bombay. I would be taking my life to Bombay— the rest of my life. There, at my bedside, there in that classroom, was the rest of my life.

NINE

LEARNING

Strength doesn't come from physical capacity. It comes from invincible will. —GANDHI

My days were filled with happiness and sadness, hope and deception, plentitude and scarcity. My life seemed to be governed by contradiction. Contradiction often seemed to govern India, too. One day everything worked out fine, and the next day nothing turned out right. Each decision seemed to carry the weight of the world, or the world's scorn. For example, I moved out of the family's house in which I had been staying, and rented one of the complex's small houses. I could put up with the rats, because the house had a mattress, a table, and a toilet, which was a luxury because it meant I wouldn't have to use the latrines. Not all the neighbors approved, however. They didn't like a white man living in the complex, especially since I was bringing in more untouchables.

I was deeply bothered on many occasions by their impressions. They questioned my professional honesty and my intentions toward their country. But I thought about the way Europeans treat immigrants in many places, so I just kept quiet. The world, especially the West, should listen and consider the views of others more often. We're not very consistent, for example, when we say we want to help developing countries and then look with disdain at the Senegalese man sleeping on the porch of a neighbor's house. We are, as Swami Prajnanpad wrote, the product of our environment. We cannot see beyond the habits and social conventions by which we are governed. "To see further, [we] must free ourselves from our interpretations." This is what I tried to do, to free myself from interpretations, to look, to observe, and to withhold judgment.

It wasn't only the locals who heaped scorn on me and the project, but also some of the elite of Indian society. After foreign embassies learned that a Spanish man was helping kids from the slums, they started calling and inviting us to dinners, which I refused as graciously as possible. One day I received a call from the French embassy. It was Nadine, my contact there: "Jaume, tonight there is a very important dinner at the Taj Mahal hotel. I have been invited. Come with me. There will be very important people that you should meet."

"Remember, I don't go to expensive restaurants even if it's an invitation. I really don't feel like it. You think it's worth it? Do you think those people would help us?"

Nadine wasn't very convinced, but pretended to be: "Of course they will help."

Such people belonged to a part of Indian society I was uncomfortable with. At times these people can be indiscreet, arrogant, and unpleasant. Yet it was difficult to turn down an opportunity to help the children.

About thirty people were at the party. On polished sand wood walls hung portraits of maharajas, who, in their time, frequented the hotel. I didn't have the proper attire, so I wore the burgundy *Punjabi kurta* the teachers had given to me. The host, an Indian multi-millionaire who owned a chain of companies (the name of which I'd rather not mention), came to meet me while a butler helped the guests find their places at the table.

"Who are you? Do you work in any embassy?" he enquired.

"My name is Jaume Sanllorente. I work for Bombay's poor."

An ostentatious laugh resonated throughout the room and the hall beyond. "You must then earn a miserable salary!" he replied, still laughing. Some of the other guests even clapped.

Nadine looked at me, ashamed. I had been right. Not only had she dragged me to the other side of the city to be with people who had nothing in common with me, but now they were all laughing at me. Dinner was pleasant, however. I was seated directly across from my host. The conversation centered on the tourism board of Switzerland and its efforts in India, about the hypnotic power of the great dictators of history, and about the changes in the world economy after 9/11.

I have to say that some of the topics were interesting, and many of the jokes were clever, but I spent the dinner in a taciturn mood. I didn't say a word. I hid my laughter when I couldn't suppress it. Meanwhile, Nadine constantly kicked me under the table.

After dinner, when guests were leaving, the host approached me. In a less strident voice he asked, "Why have you been so serious all night? Maybe you didn't like the food?"

"The food was delicious. I loved it, thank you so much," I told him without much enthusiasm.

"And so, why have you been so serious?"

Nadine listened with curiosity, as the big-bellied host stood firmly in front of me waiting for a reply. "Well . . ." I answered, "you said before we had dinner that my bosses must pay me miserably. But considering that my bosses, Bombay's untouchables, pay me with smiles, how can I betray their interests at such a splendid dinner?"

Several guests who were at the door turned around. The next day the host sent me a note on company stationery: "Please accept my apologies and give this to your bosses."

Attached was a coupon for three outfits of clothes for each child, including clothing for the monsoons. That same week we received donations from other guests. A week later, an editor at the *Times of India* published an article titled "The Spanish Robin Hood," in which she praised our project. The praise was exaggerated, yet beneficial for the orphanage's development.

AND SO I SPENT my days attending to orphanage business and learning Hindi. The children laughed a lot each time I spoke their language, and they imitated me. And I imitated them using their Spanish expressions. I could see that they were happy. We already had one hundred kids, plus sixty more from the surrounding area attended classes at the orphanage.

The first sentence I learned in Hindi was "I am not from Alibag." Alibag is a town south of Bombay whose inhabitants are thought to be not too bright, especially by those living in Bombay. As with many sayings, this one has little merit, if any at all. The phrase means something like "Don't take me for a fool," and it's very useful when bargaining. In that part of the world, a Caucasian often represents to a native the opportunity for extracting a little extra money out of a transaction, as it were— yet I didn't find this the case at all in my dealings.

The children thought my little phrase very funny, and when we had our first camping trip in Khandala, a few hours from Bombay, they made me say it to every person we met. I also learned to speak English with an Indian accent, since no one could understand me otherwise. Fortunately my English was good to start with, so it wasn't hard.

In June the sky exploded with monsoon rains. The compound was flooded, and the children couldn't get to school. The world outside seemed a fountain, a flowing, falling, rushing fountain. I had to run anytime I went outside to see the children. My photo album no longer served as my Duracell battery. The children, themselves, provided me with warmth and affection in the middle of the monsoon—offered me rays of sunshine with their smiles.

Learning

Each day I was learning to be more generous, to love without limits, to give without expecting anything in return, to have a solid and rooted sense of words, to appreciate each day's small things, to listen, to observe, to see. We didn't always have electricity, and sometimes neighbors stole the water from our cistern. We spent entire days without lights or water.

I realized how Western amenities are taken for granted, for example, turning on a computer or a bug zapper. Despite the rains, I had to keep moving forward my promotional and legislative agendas in Spain. Some people complained that I didn't answer their e-mails. They had no way of knowing that the nearest coffee shop with an Internet connection was an hour away; even then, flooding often got in the way.

Night came early and without diversion. The city was two hours away, impossible to get to in the rains. I would read myself to sleep by candlelight. Mosquitoes and rats kept me company; some nights I could hear a cobra outside. One day we found one underneath a sofa where several of the girls slept.

Despite such inconveniences, I adapted to the solitude of rural life there in the valley. I learned to live with nature, to observe, to listen, and to appreciate the elegant movement of bushes in the wind. I began to detect melodies in the crickets' incessant concerts, to refresh my face with the morning's dew. To discover all this and to know that I was part of it was an indescribable feeling; it was sustaining. We are surrounded by miracles. And we are blind to them.

The bureaucracy, on the other hand, was a nightmare. Every thirty days, I had to stand in long lines to pay the electricity, water, and rental bills for the little houses —always in cash. Mail was eternally late in arriving, and there were always complications. My patience and sense of humor became more refined; I needed both to survive.

One time they called me from customs. We had received from Spain some big boxes containing notebooks for the children. When I went to pick them up, the officials asked for money. I didn't want to pay because I knew it would just go to line their pockets. They pretended they didn't see me, and each time I talked they teased me, saying that they had heard a strange noise, asking themselves what it could be. I spent nine hours in that office, sitting on the floor, singing, and reciting poems like a crazy person. Finally they gave me the boxes—I suppose because they didn't want to listen to me anymore. Fortitude became a blessing.

With time, I grasped the system, short cuts and efficient methods for advancing my cause and the children's.

Of course not every policeman in India is corrupt. Fortunately, an increasing number of people feel a strong ethical sensibility, a sense of duty toward their fellow man and woman. Criticism is often justified and is necessary for overcoming barriers to citizenship. But criticism is most useful when it is constructive criticism—real solutions to problems.

The reason nonprofit organizations first emerged was because governments were unable or unwilling to help their citizens. Apathy and stupidity in government have made NGOs necessary. Yet it might be time for NGOs to push for change, to seek greater opportunities for helping others, for helping the disenfranchised. It's more useful to work alongside governmental organizations, seeking synergies that serve the needs of the people, rather than to simply criticize those organizations while trying to carry on independently. Let's stop wasting time arguing over how to paint the wall. Let's just paint it.

DESPITE THE DIFFICULTY at the orphanage, despite the gloomy weather, our accounts were looking up, and I saw that we could take in more children and perhaps send them to better schools. Yet I knew that I shouldn't express enthusiasm so quickly, for experience had taught me that reversals in fortune, both financial and emotional, were common.

One evening after doing the accounts, I heard the door bell ringing incessantly. I opened the door to a tall man about fifty years old who looked me up and down with an inexpressive face.

"Does Jaume sir live in this house?" he asked in Hindi.

"Yes, that's me," I answered in his language.

He looked at me again from head to toe, this time with disdain.

"Do not touch what shouldn't be touched. Move back to your country. We do not need help. Leave us alone, and don't fill the neighborhood with garbage."

Before I could answer, he spit on my face and then stayed there without moving. I cleaned his saliva from my face and observed my hand. "Water for hope," I answered, surprising myself with my reaction. Perhaps astonished by my response, he turned and left. I thought about how I could help that man if I ever saw him again. How could I make him happier? I had to work harder to win the hearts and minds of my neighbors in light of their opposition to an influx of more untouchables and inferior castes into the neighborhood.

Learning

There are no enemies. An enemy is a friend who needs help. If we help him, everyone wins: The world has another happy person, and the happy person has another friend.

TEN

EVERYONE'S GOD

There is only one God. And he has no enemies.
—GURU NANAK

One good day, Karmayog's Vinay Somani called. He had been the first person to talk to me about Kartika's Home, on my trip that seemed a thousand years ago. Vinay told me how pleased he was about his decision to put me in contact with the orphanage and also explained that there was another school in crisis: Yashodhan. It was located in the Shastri Nagar hills, west of Thane, on the outskirts of Bombay, where the shacks multiply until the top of the mountains. The school had five hundred children from the age of three to eighteen; most were from the slums. It was closing, and the children were being put on the street, where they would be forced to beg.

In my view, education is the key to solving the problems of the untouchables, of the poor, in India. They must be set free, and the only way to set these people free is to break the chains of ignorance. Some people think that charity alone is the solution to poverty, yet, as Muhammad Yunus wrote, "Stripping poor people of initiative only perpetuates the problem. It allows us to pursue our own lives without worrying about the poor, serving only our consciences."

Breaking the chains begins with us, with our enabling those enslaved. I thought it necessary from the start at the orphanage, for example, to offer new employees, especially cleaning ladies and cooks, free education, whether at the orphanage or at another school. If they chose the latter we gave them financial help in addition to salaries.

Perhaps it was fate that I had been approached about Yashodhan. We had only just finished ironing out many of the wrinkles related to the Diplomatic school, which we had opened thanks to the generous contribution of an American company. This school is a big, beautiful structure of solid materials set in a field in front of the orphanage. American architects and engineers supervised the construction. I think we set the Guinness world record for the completion of a building, especially in India.

Slowly, we filled the school with students; after a few months almost five hundred children were enrolled. Making the school function properly was difficult. It was extremely complicated organizing registration and keeping proper records. Most of the staff had never used a computer and were unaccustomed to working under pressure. But I always preferred to hire local staff rather than bringing in foreign volunteers. Inclusive development was my guiding vision.

Despite the difficulties, our school progressed rapidly. Families increasingly trusted us, and we were making gains controlling absentecism, which had gotten out of control the first months. We put one person in charge of visiting the homes of the children who didn't come to school two or three days in a row without an excuse. Often the cause was the construction of a building near their homes, in which case every child, including the three year olds, was put to work by their fathers. A child in school is lost income, so the competition for the children's time was fierce.

It was important for me to memorize the names of the new pupils during the first months after the opening of the Diplomatic school. They came each morning in their uniforms, looking frightened but ready for lessons. We also hired more teachers and paid them well so they

wouldn't leave for other schools in Bombay, where salaries were better. It mattered that our teachers were first-
rate. We needed to uphold our image. We chose Sujit
for director of the school. He was already at Kartika's
Home when I first visited the orphanage. I also hired his
wife, Sharina, as my assistant. A logistics director was
hired for Kartika's Home, too, to keep the orphanage
independent from the school.

There were two other schools in the area besides the
Diplomatic school: a public school that consisted of a
one hundred square foot room surrounded by four mud
walls, and a private school that was too expensive for
families in the valley—they had enough difficulty simply putting food on the table.

We tried to offer all of the amenities of a private
school. During the final stretch, we took turns visiting every corner of the region touting the school and its
opening. We established official tuition fees, but families paid what they could. Tuition fees are important
because people don't want to think that their children
attend a school for "the poor." Making them see that education is valuable is also important. We used only the
best promotional material, only what the elite schools
might use. We wanted everything to be top quality,
from the cornerstone of the building to the corner of-

fice for the principal, from the books to the instruction itself.

We applied the same principles to donated clothing. Ripped and worn-out clothing from Spain was thrown out: I personally threw out clothing that was filthy or torn. We only kept what we would have given to our own children. I've always found the word "charity" repugnant. It suggests inferiority. "Help," on the other hand, suggests equality.

The school was no exception. Those children should receive the same education that my father would have liked for me, or that I would wish for my own children.

The situation at Yashodhan was similar to the one at Kartika's Home orphanage, déjà vu in some respects, and I already had experience running a school. So I decided I would help the parents at Yashodhan: I would not allow the school to disappear; I would cover their debts and pay the teachers' salaries. I would help those children have a better future.

It was not easy to find the necessary permits. It took us a year to get authorization from Delhi, including the Foreign Currency Regulation Act permit required for an Indian organization to receive foreign aid.

To be a biological orphan is well understood in India. To be a religious orphan is inconceivable. All the teachers at Yashodhan and most of its students were Hindu. I was obsessed with respecting each person's religion, because we can help others only from a position of respect, never by imposing out own views.

When we opened the Diplomatic school we decided to respect each person's religion and to offer classes in ethics and behavior. Eighty percent of Indians are Hindu, but in Bombay many religions coexist, and many of those religions are stronger in Bombay than in other parts of the country. I suppose this matrix was inherited from British colonialism (Christianity) and from the fact that the religious orders which remained after independence opened the first religious education schools in Bombay.

Throughout history many congregations have offered help, but with, it seems to me, coercion: "We will help you, but you have to accept our way of life and beliefs." Their help was conditional. Yet a large number of religious people have never tried to change the beliefs of those whom they help. They have extended their hand to the needy, following the internal command of their kind souls and not the obligations imposed by their beliefs. A good example is Father Federico Sopeña, who has lived in Bombay for many years, and whom I admire deeply for his work for the Adivasi Indian indigenous people. This was our approach at Diplomatic: we decided not to impose conditions, because there was nothing to preach, no dogma to reinforce.

One thing I had learned from my first trip to India was that I needed to better understand the numerous beliefs, religions, and doctrines of the country. Hindus (by the way, Indians do not like people to call every Indian a Hindu, because not all Indians follow Hinduism) believe in Brahman, the god of the eternal and absolute, that is, "God" with a capital *G*. From there, different manifestations emerge: those are the multitude of worshiped gods. Brahman is usually portrayed in three forms, Vishnu, Brahma, and Shiva.

Vishnu is the one who protects, who brings good things. He is usually portrayed with four arms, carrying a lotus flower (the world being revealed), a conch (its internal vibration is the same as the cosmos, from which all beings emerge), a disk, and a mace (which he triumphantly got after vanquishing Indra, the goddess of battles). Vishnu, whose spouse is Lakshmi, has twenty-two reincarnations, including Krishna and Rama. Shiva is the destroyer, but Hindus believe that his existence enabled the possibility of creation. His creative function is symbolized by the *lingam*, a phallic portrait worshiped in many temples around the country. Shiva, who has 1008 names, is also portrayed as the lord of yoga, his body covered in ashes and with a third, "wisdom," eye. Serpents coil around his body, and he rides, armed with his trident, on top of the bull Nandi. Shiva's spouse is Parvati, who can also inhabit several shapes.

Christian Indians disapprove of the worship of so many gods. They are not the only ones. Sikhs do not admit idolatry of so many figures either, even if they are much more respectful of Hindu beliefs. Approximately nineteen million Sikhs live in India. They come from Punjab, in the north of the country, where the guru Nanak founded the religion at the end of the fifteenth century. Sikhism emerged from opposition to the Hindu caste system, and sought to incorporate the best parts of Hinduism and Islam. Sikh's sacred text is the *Guru Granth Sahib*, and the belief in an elected race of soldiers who follow a strict code of moral conduct is essential.

There are five *kakars* (emblems and rules) for every Sikh: *kesh* (beard and long hair, symbolizing immortality), *khanga* (ornamental comb to keep the long hair), *kaccha* (pants that symbolize modesty), *kirpan* (a small saber or sword representing power), and *kada* (metallic bracelet worn on the right wrist, symbolizing courage). It is easy then to recognize Sikhs by the turbans they wear. At the school, I could always guess their religion by their last name, because it usually contained the component *"singh"* (which means lion). Sikhs are known as excellent negotiators and great businessmen.

I also had developed friendships with some Jainists. Around five million people practice that minority religion in India. It was founded by Mahavira (a contemporary of Buddha) in the sixth century B.C. Jainists believe one can only go forward with a pure soul. They practice nonviolence to the utmost expression. Many times they carry small brooms to sweep the floor ahead of themselves, to be sure not to step on any animal. They cover their mouths so as not to swallow an insect by mistake, thereby cutting its life short.

I noticed as well the increasing number of Buddhists among the *dalit* communities, or untouchables. The number of followers of Siddhartha's doctrines increased considerably in the 1950s, and their number continues to grow today, especially among the followers of Dr. B. R. Ambedkar, one of the first activists to put his political power to work for *dalits*.

IN 1908, DR. AMBEDKAR became the first member of the Mahar caste—an untouchable caste from Andhra Pradesh—to graduate from Elphinstone College in Bombay. Succeeding at such a prestigious academic institution in spite of his social level was an extraordinary accomplishment.

After graduating, he traveled to the United States, where he studied economics at Columbia University. He then studied law in London and returned to India in 1923 with more than ten years of postgraduate education. In 1935 he declared that he "wouldn't die as a Hindu," and began looking for a nondiscriminatory religion. From then on, until his death in 1956, Dr. Ambedkar explored converting to various religions, including Sikhism, Christianity, and Islam.

Shortly before his death, Dr. Ambedkar converted to Buddhism. The ceremony took place in Nagpur and half a million *dalits* attended. Most of them converted to Buddhism that same day.

CHRISTIAN TEACHERS at the Diplomatic school expressed displeasure when they learned that the new school, Yashodhan, was Hindu, and that I, myself, was a champion of respecting the codes and guidelines established by the families at that school. I always tried to humor them without giving offense. If, for example, my Christian assistant said that she would read the Bible to try to find solutions for some of our difficult projects, I asked her to also find someone to pray to Allah and the Hindu gods, too. And if there weren't enough people to pray, I asked her to give me the extra gods and I would pray to them. This disturbed her, but through diplomacy and jokes I usually was able to calm everyone down.

It was the same with bonuses: I started giving them to Hindu employees around the days of Diwali, the Festival of Lights (October and November), and I gave Christians theirs at Christmastime.

Paradoxically, as my mistrust of religions increased, my connection with divinity grew as well. More and more, I felt the existence of God. And so my experiences in India took me away from organized religion but closer to God. I find it difficult to believe in religions that divide humanity.

On one occasion, a furious Christian Indian said to me, "How can you say that you respect all religions? Doesn't your father have only one name and don't you have only one father? How can you then defend the existence of one God with different names?"

"Look," I said, "only one God exists. People have given him various names. It's true, I have only one father, but it's also true that you yourself have another one, who is not the same as mine. Yet that doesn't imply that one or the other is undeserving of our love."

Little by little, I came to the conclusion that my relationship to India was similar to that of a husband who is hopelessly in love with his wife: he coddles and grovels and spoils but never understands. I will die deeply in love with India, and I will know a lot about her, but I will not have understood her. In any case, it would be pretentious to think that one could understand India in all its complexity—or any country for that matter.

That complexity extended to language. The Diplomatic school, for example, was becoming a Tower of Babel. Kids were coming from the north of Bombay who spoke only Urdu. The administrative staff spoke English and Marathi. I spoke English and Hindi. So we had many languages in the same room, with no one really understanding the others. Meanwhile, many mothers at the school were covered in black burkas. They never looked at me or others when they were speaking or when spoken to. One could barely see their eyes. I learned not to look at them when talking so as not to insult them. It was difficult enough just getting them to enroll their children at the school.

In spite of disputes among teachers, and other general problems involved in running a school, everything seemed to be going well at the Diplomatic school. But one day, without warning, the owner of one of the little houses that we rented notified us that he was selling the house and that the children would have to leave within a few days. He didn't care whether the children had a place to go, or even a roof over their heads.

That same night, the children slept in my house, and I slept on a bench in one of the gardens. To sleep under that starry dome, knowing that the children were safe, was a gift. Around midnight I heard someone crying. I saw the shadow of a man sitting on a nearby bench.

"What is it?" I asked.

"I am finished, I want to die . . ."

I went to him and tried to console him. His face was familiar, probably someone living in the area that I saw every morning.

"Can I help you?" I insisted.

"I had to close my business, and I am broke. My daughter left last year for the United States and abandoned our two grandsons. My wife and I take care of them. We don't have anything left. I don't know how we will keep sending the children to school . . ."

I explained to him about the schools I managed. I told him not to worry, that I would do whatever I could to help, and I assured him that his grandchildren would keep studying.

"I know very well who you are," he said. "Don't you recognize me?"

It was the same man who some months before had knocked on my door and spit on my face. He knelt and cried in despair. I helped him to his feet and smiled at him. He had found help, and I had found a friend.

Something magical also happened the day I was invited to Yashodhan to celebrate the decision to save the school. Hindus believe that rain outside of the monsoon season brings good luck. Destiny arranged it so that, at the precise moment I arrived in front of the school door in the small square, it began to rain—in May, the driest season of all.

Everyone was happy. Many people threw themselves at my feet and caressed them and then touched their hearts. Those were the student's mothers, some of whom couldn't stop crying. But they were tears of happiness. Boys and girls threw orange petals from the roof tops, and the village's doors had been decorated with *rangolis*—beautiful drawings made with rice dust that are put in homes during celebrations to keep bad gods away and give light to the good ones.

"Right now," said Yashodhan's director, "you are their god." Three bands struck up celebratory music. Mothers pushed their way forward in the crowd to caress my feet. Their gratitude made me uncomfortable. That night I wrote a letter to a friend saying that, in India, I am either spat on as the enemy or treated as a demi-god. It can be unnerving, especially for someone unprepared for such receptions. I adapted with time, though. I became accustomed to the praise but didn't take it for granted. I tried to remain focused, for I knew that in India there was more misery and tragedy than joy. And I was about to encounter both once again.

AMONG THE NEW CHILDREN at the Diplomatic school, Ramesh stuck out most. Seven years old, he was as bulky as a twelve-year-old. It was unusual to see such a big kid in a place where most children were thin. I was very fond of Ramesh and I think he was fond of me. Every morning before classes, he gobbled a *vada pav* in the lunchroom. I made room for one, too, even though I had eaten breakfast earlier. Ramesh's family lived in a shack about ten minutes away from school. He and his two brothers were always impeccably dressed, and their uniforms, bought with donations from Spain, were well cared for.

One sunny day in November my assistant, Sharmila, came running into my office: "I just heard horrifying news! Something terrible has happened! It's Ramesh. They found his body floating on a Vasai raft."

Apparently, he had disappeared on Sunday and his family had found him dead that morning. I was told he had been bitten by a snake while strolling along the river and was knocked into the water. I ran to his house, but of course there was nothing I could do. In that world everyone was or seemed accustomed to death. For me it was tragic and devastating. Yet in India, where tragedy and devastation reign, death—when it comes—is less unexpected.

I could think only of how joyful Ramesh was, how agreeable, talkative, and even mischievous. For example, one day I had found him crying in the hall. He wouldn't calm down so that we could understand what had happened. Finally, when we were about to leave for his house, Ramesh had uttered, "I lost my sock." We looked at his feet, saw one white sock, and couldn't stop laughing. Ramesh didn't want the other students to see him without his sock, so we had to hide him in the office until another pair was found. (Not only had one of Ramesh's socks vanished, but also his records. For weeks we couldn't find his enrollment papers.) His actions were very impressive, as he made sure no one saw him walk in or out of my office without both socks on.

ELEVEN

COMING BACK TO LIFE

An important part of the job of raising the
quality of life of leprous patients is building the
foundation to help them improve their social
position. —RAMASWAMI GANAPATI

I suffered several serious asthma attacks in a short time,
perhaps because of my increasing activity outside of
the orphanage. So I checked into Holy Spirit hospital in
Andheri. No sooner had I been put on a stretcher than
a woman recognized me. She told me about a man who
lived in a nearby slum and who was having great difficulty because he had lost his job and had two small children to support.

So many people in Bombay needed help, and our
organization had limited resources. I had to learn to
say no, even though it was very difficult—especially
when, for example, desperate mothers put their babies

141

in my arms and tried to get me to take them away. I initially told the woman no, but then I thought about all the administrative work that awaited me back at the orphanage, all the lines I had to stand in at various governmental and city offices. I took my oxygen mask off and said, "Tell him to come see me in three days."

Meanwhile, the almost daily visits to the slums were taking their toll and gave me much cause for reflection. It was clear that I couldn't keep building orphanages. There weren't sufficient resources or manpower. Also, more and more I was working to avoid separating children from their families. I began giving priority to children sold by their families to prostitution rings. It was important that children with kind parents should remain at home. The question was how to give those children the possibility of a better future? It wasn't only about saving people from the fire, but about extinguishing the fire.

I thought there must be a way of helping them, of educating them, without taking them away from their homes. Not all parents wanted to amputate their children's limbs or sell them into prostitution. They were poor, not criminals. I found the writings of Amartya Sen immensely helpful during this time, especially his intelligent contributions to the study of poverty, in which he particularly points out the enormous latent potential within each man and woman. We are all equal; some of us just have more opportunities to develop our abilities.

Three days after I got out of the hospital, a slight man with a moustache came to my house. He was the man who had lost his job and who needed to support his children. His name was Vinay and he was ready to do whatever I asked of him. He has been at my side ever since. Vinay is a model of self-sufficiency. A man who owned one pair of shoes, who lived in a shack and hadn't had the opportunity to go to school, now had a job that wasn't collecting garbage. Today he is an outstanding worker, able to deal easily with government officials and to accomplish administrative tasks flawlessly. And why shouldn't he be an outstanding worker? Why shouldn't he be able to accomplish administrative tasks? The question is why the question has to be asked.

A few days before Vinay appeared in my life, a journalist asked me, "When will the untouchables of India be self-sufficient?"

I answered with a question: "When will we allow them to be so?" I was interested in breaking down barriers, in bringing out the human in human beings and helping them become who they are.

My interest extended to leprous people who lived in the Vasai Road station, where I caught the train to go from Vasai to the slums. The presence of leprosy was overwhelming, but it seemed that the world had somehow forgotten the disease, as if it no longer existed. I had first visited a leprosy center two years before. It was located in the same area, a few miles from the orphanage. I was enormously influenced, even shocked, by what I saw. It wasn't the sight of lepers, but the solitude and neglect that I felt in their hearts that most disturbed me.

Particularly sad were some very young patients with desolate expressions, without any life in their eyes, confined and isolated. I felt I was in a different world, outside life or death. It wasn't heaven or hell, but an uncomfortable, silent limbo. In between the two rows of iron beds that filled the big room, I noticed a face, destroyed by the illness. I instinctively approached; the man was gazing at me with moist eyes.

"Who is he?"

"His name is Kunal. He is thirteen years old. His parents abandoned him. His illness was already advanced by the time we found him. He now lives here, and it seems that his leprosy is stable. We are treating him with a multi-drug therapy."

"Multi-drug therapy," I repeated, realizing how ignorant I was. I was surprised at the distortion the illness had produced on that boy's face; I hadn't even realized how young he was.

I soon began visiting the leprosy centers more often, sometimes taking visitors from Barcelona, like Verónica Blume, the model, who is a great friend of the project. I also began to study the illness, consulting specialists, visiting libraries, bookshops . . . I learned that even in medical circles leprosy is believed to have been cured.

At the same time, I continued to think about how we could help children get an education rather than see them taken out of school because they had to work. I consulted the programs established in Brazil in the mid 1990s, which gave fixed payments to poor families as incentives to send their children to school. The program was called Stipend for Schooling and was included within the minimum wage programs established in Brazil in 1995.

The first proposal emerged in Brasilia, where the governor announced the program's establishment. It stipulated that any family with children seven to fourteen years old and which earned less than half the minimal wage could receive a monthly payment that would bring their income up to the minimum wage, as long as their children's attendance rate at school was above 90 percent.

The program, which was soon replicated in other states of Brazil, also attempted to reduce child labor, since the payment would cover income the family lost because the child was no longer working. It would also increase the level of school attendance among poor families, which would reduce poverty over the long term. In this way, education would be the main tool to break the circle of poverty. Such programs, with compensation tied to education, have had a sizable effect on social and educational reforms in South America.

What could be offered to poor families in Bombay? If we developed a barter system with a direct monetary benefit for the families, the extortion networks would just increase their pressure on the area and everything could fall apart. The challenge was to find a formula that directly benefited families without giving them money.

These two projects, addressing leprosy and the need to keep children in school—occupied a large part of my life. But it was my visits to the leper colonies that got me thinking more critically about how I could help. Soon thereafter, "Coming Back to Life" was formed, dedicated to the academic and social reintegration of leprosy patients and their children. The project involved expanding the circumference of the NGO; until then it had been centered on children and their education. I spent days thinking about Kunal. What could he expect to find outside the lugubrious hall of the leprosy center once he was cured? How could he advance in a society that would always reject him for the marks that injustice had drawn on his skin?

Sufferers of leprosy are stigmatized and demonized in India. Many cured patients are rejected by their families, and they rarely find jobs. They have no recourse but to live on the street and beg, forever victims of poverty and scorn. Their loved ones fare no better. Many children of leprous patients are rejected by schools because of their parent's illness, for fear of contagion.

The project was about to be launched when problems began. Seventy percent of all leprosy patients live in India, yet even within my own team in Bombay, people rejected those suffering from the illness. These colleagues threatened to withdraw from the organization if I started helping the sick. Nevertheless, by then I had learned that, despite obstacles, nothing is impossible if one dreams with strength and purpose. Just thinking about Kunal being able to work and contributing to society kept me going.

Then destiny introduced Dr. Ramaswami Ganapati, vice-president of the Society for the Eradication of Leprosy and founder of the Bombay Leprosy Project, whose impeccable career path had made him an important man in India. My neighbors criticized me the first day I met him because they didn't want an organization in their neighborhood getting involved with leprosy. Despite this opposition, Dr. Ganapati and I met frequently and discovered synergies between his organization and Bombay Smiles.

We both rejected the notion that leprosy colonies were necessary. We both rejected the position of hospitals, which wouldn't treat the sick. We wanted leprosy patients to have access to treatment at regular hospitals; we rejected discrimination. I will never be able to thank Dr. Ganapati enough for understanding and respecting my tenacity.

In collaboration with Dr. Ganapati and his team, directed by Dr. Pai, we laid the foundation for "Coming Back to Life," which is composed of three parts:

First, there is a program of financial aid to individuals, which pays for tuition and books as well as accessories, not only for patients, but also for their children who have been denied access to an education due to the leprosy in the family. Next, I offered Bombay Leprosy Project the use of space in our offices, which would become the epicenter of a program covering northern Bombay, especially the outskirts. Organized tours could be arranged from this office to detect early-stage leprosy cases in time to stop the illness from destroying a patient and his or her family. Finally, Bombay Smiles supported the salaries of parents of leprosy patients and leprosy patients themselves who were beneficiaries of Coming Back to Life. Kunal didn't have to be a statue in a dormitory full of despair any longer.

Once Coming Back to Life was off the ground, I could focus on the project for ensuring children's education. I continued to explore Brazil's approach to the problem.

And then something interesting occurred.

I HAD BEEN TAKING Lakshmi's mother (the woman with the festering leg I had met during my first trip) to the doctor ever since I had returned to Bombay. It had been very difficult to find a hospital that would treat her. Money didn't even work, because she was an untouchable. I finally got in to see Dr. Chetan Oberai, an eminent dermatologist with a private practice in Lilavati, the most expensive hospital in the city.

Although the woman's leg still looked pretty bad, the wounds were healing and there was no longer a danger of infection. Observing that I had gone to the hospital with her and that she was getting treatment, her neighbors in Dharavi started to ask me for help as well. In many instances, they didn't tell the truth about their ailments. Unfortunately the social status of entering a prestigious hospital was often more important than getting medical assistance. Nor did I care whether they told me the truth, because a strategy for getting them to gradually enroll their children in school was forming in my mind.

What if we could offer them health instead of money? I asked myself. I began drafting the proposal for a project called "A Card of Hope." Each card entitled a family to medical treatment, including routine checkups, visits to doctors, and necessary surgical interventions and treatments. In return, families had to sign a contract agreeing to put their children through school and to stop pressuring them to work before they finished their studies. If the children were absent without cause and the family did not comply with the agreement, all benefits would be lost and the beneficiaries obliged to pay a percentage of the medical services previously received.

We are now conducting pilot projects with families in Dharavi and Andheri. Obviously there are many obstacles, for example, enrollment: Many families come from other parts of India and have left behind their children's registration papers. It is difficult to enroll a child in school if that child doesn't officially "exist." Even so, the pilot project is providing insight into how to give the children of Bombay access to a healthy future, one that includes an education.

TWELVE

NORMALITY

We will not be able to change society if we do not first change ourselves. It is human beings—all of us —who have created those societies generation after generation. —KRISHNAMURTI

We began accepting paying students to the Diplomatic school once it had been open for a while. We adhered to our initial policy of hiring only the best teachers. Our curriculum included math, English, and numerous afterschool activities, similar to other Indian schools of quality.

At first it was difficult to enroll children from wealthier families, because they would have to interact with untouchables. Yet we succeeded, the importance of a good education prevailing. I was very happy not to have created a "school for the poor," but rather an exemplary educational institution where quality was paramount.

In just one year the Diplomatic School became financially self-sufficient. Indeed, it was soon able to transfer money to Kartika's Home, which would never again have to rely on outside funding and would remain independent. In spite of such positive steps, it was difficult for all of us to "let go" of Kartika's Home; it had been under our umbrella for so long. But we understood the benefits of independence and growth, and how they lead to freedom. Helping means eventually opening the cage so the bird can fly away and be free, rather than keeping it captive for the rest of its life.

We were now able to redirect donors' contributions to new projects developed with local partners—organizations created autonomously by individual communities of Bombay which would benefit directly from them. Such projects would be able to rely on the best of foundations: the dictates and needs of the city's population, to which we devoted our energies.

The first project that we developed with Indian communities was the establishment of one hundred kindergartens—*balwadis*—for three thousand preschoolers from the slums, children between two and six years old. This program, which continues to this day, aims to break the vicious circle of poverty and lack of education. Very often we would take in an eight- or nine-year-old girl, rescued from a brothel. The child would not know how to read or write, and could not be put in a class with other children her age.

We wanted to rescue these children as early as possible so they wouldn't be so thoroughly disadvantaged. We wanted to provide them with a good education at a young age because we also wanted to enroll them in good Bombay schools once they reached the right age.

In addition to an education, each child daily receives a nutritious meal. Bombay Smiles is very conscientious about the complexities of life in the slums; we are sensitive to families' situations and social contexts. We understand how difficult it is for different families to meet even the most basic needs of their children. Yet we are aware that we, too, must fail. We are realists and recognize that our contributions are small and aren't meeting all of the children's needs. But we're having an impact, and this project is one example.

Thanks to all the people in the world that support us, these children and others have the opportunity to receive an early education and meals appropriate to their age at least five days a week. It is a small gesture in the context of the tens of millions of Indian children in despairing situations, but each healthy child, excited about access to a primary education, is a child to whom vital choices are given from the beginning. And one life, one life only, is everything.

We have received donations from around the world, but the increased interest shown in our work from many parts of Spain made me think that our headquarters should be there. Today Bombay Smiles consists of a team—just enough people not to waste resources—of efficient and committed individuals who work to meet the standards of our partners' contributions. This team works daily to transform resources into a better quality of life for thousands of untouchables in Bombay.

I have always wanted to keep Bombay Smiles a small, family-like entity—professional, persevering, and ambitious, but also intimate, tangible, and transparent. Thus, the organization has one person per department, which helps to avoid waste and ensure that the majority of contributions go directly to Bombay's poor and untouchables.

My views on my role within Bombay Smiles have changed considerably in recent years. In the beginning I remember always wanting to be directly involved in the children's education and health: teaching, caring for the sick, playing with the children. Then one day I realized that my direct intervention was no longer necessary, that I might become a hindrance. I remember the day I told myself: Jaume, you pretend to help out of respect, and so you mingle here and there. Is this necessary? Why do you want to teach first grade if they have capable teachers already? Why do you want to care for the sick and complete nursing classes if the Bombay Leprosy Project has highly qualified personnel?

I slowly began reconfiguring my role within the organization, always aiming to serve projects without meddling in their development. I tried overseeing projects rather than, say, interfering with jobs where I was not needed. Now, my job is more about logistics, a never-ending succession of meetings, trips, and talks, as well as constant training and the solving of bureaucratic problems. Each section of a project must be administered by qualified staff, but most important, at least for Bombay Smiles, people must be local, that is, Indian.

Our volunteers must also be Indian. I am sure that in more rural areas, or perhaps where there is less support and infrastructure, working with expatriates is sometimes positive. In Bombay, however, where it is easy to find a good teacher, a good nutritionist, or a good doctor among its twenty million inhabitants, there is no point in having foreign volunteers.

Had we agreed to take on every volunteer who offered, more than three hundred people from local communities in Bombay would not have the jobs they have today. Undoubtedly, Bombay Smiles is a fantastic resource, and a way to engage the community, to get it involved in a project—which is as necessary for its development as water is for a plant.

It is important for foreigners to understand that Bombay is not a poor place, but a place with many poor. The city has hospitals, universities, drugstores, and so on —which is all the more tragic because more than half of Bombay's population doesn't have access to these places. I always tell Americans, when I am in the United States, that the projects we support are in the Bronx of Bombay. They understand such a statement: The Bronx is a symbol of a terribly poor and miserable area in the heart of New York.

It was also important to count on a couple of "right-hand" people in India, collaborators who had my confidence. The highly qualified personnel in Bombay have enabled me to spend longer periods in Barcelona where my father, my grandmother, and my lifelong friends live. It would have been somehow wrong to develop a project based on love and not to start within my own home.

Just as I have tried to tap into each person's potential, I have learned to profit from my profile as a journalist by collaborating with the media and re-establishing institutional relationships that might help our beneficiaries. I have never ceased to feel like a journalist. Indeed, I am a journalist now more than ever. I have directed the world's attention—at least those willing to listen—to the pitiful and difficult environment in Bombay in which millions of untouchables live.

We also have developed what we call "awareness platforms." We want to further the world's awareness of Bombay's poor, 60 percent of Bombay's inhabitants. We want these platforms to serve as bridges between international sponsors and Indian communities, even in instances where Bombay Smiles is not directly involved. It is important to join forces in this common fight with poverty. I still do not understand the rivalries among NGOs—so much time is lost in such conflicts.

Above all, in my life I have tried to maintain normality. I have tried to be the normal person who spends long periods of time in the West, mingling with people his own age, going out, laughing, working like any other person. I have tried to get out from under that mystical halo associated with so many social workers. I am not religious; I am not a mystic, nor a master. Each day, I feel more ignorant. I do not spend my days levitating in an orphanage; I work hard every day like any other person, in my case to increase equality and possibilities for Bombay's poorest people.

And when I am invited to give a talk or attend a conference, I try not to preach or moralize. Instead, I try to describe my experiences, simply and straightforwardly. I want my listeners to understand that a normal human being, one without special virtues, one without extraordinary spiritual connections, can help to make the world better.

THIRTEEN

THE PRICE OF LOVE

Death is like life, when one knows how to live. It is impossible to live without simultaneously dying. It is impossible to live without psychologically dying every minute. —KRISHNAMURTI

New successes brought new failures. Neighbors at the development where the orphanage was housed disapproved of the increasing number of untouchables and children from the slums. They soon started blaming us for sewer odors and for lack of a healthy environment in the area. Of course their assertions were absurd. Arguments between certain members of local parties made it clear that it would be wise to create a legal entity under which all of our projects would operate. This entity was to be called Bombay Smiles. Once again we had to endure lines at governmental offices; once again we met with numerous bureaucratic obstructions; once again we encountered countless obstacles.

I also had to deal with individuals whose weaknesses included untrustworthiness and fraud—fortunately nothing serious. It goes without saying that I was constantly vigilant about rooting out fraud. "Rob a bank and not starving children," I once said to an employee whose intentions were dubious. In spite of these obstacles, each disappointment and each effort was accompanied by the satisfaction and joy of what had already been achieved. Our project had become famous throughout India, especially among the people of Bombay. With all the accolades, however, came recriminations and threats. The number of children at the orphanage was growing. Many of them came from Kamathipura and the prostitution houses, which meant lost revenue for organized crime. Extortion rackets in Dharavi were also angry at us: fewer families were being exploited. Increasingly I was receiving threats, and once our office was set on fire.

One day, a colleague came into my office and said that the Bombay police were on the phone. I had no idea what they wanted but they summoned me to Andheri's police station. They were exquisitely kind, which was surprising. I had wanted to talk to them for some time, especially regarding children from Kamathipura. I arrived in Andheri and two officers showed me into a dingy office lacking any charm whatsoever.

"We need to talk to you about a delicate matter."

"Please, inspector, go on."

"Last week we raided two apartments in Grant Road. They belong to *X*, someone who, as you may know, is the head of numerous kidnapping rackets in Dharavi and Kamathipura."

"Yes, a major-league pimp. But what am I here for? I actually wanted to ask for your help because . . ."

"You are in danger. Your name is written more than once in some documents that we seized."

"Yes, of course, they must not like our work, but that's all. Is this why you called me?"

For a moment, I felt as if I were in a police movie, at the whim of the police. I was becoming impatient. The inspector continued:

"Your life is in danger. I am positive. You have two options. You either carry a gun or hire a guard. If you would like, we can send a police car to guard your house for a while."

"What are you saying?" I asked. "How can I carry a gun or be guarded? And do we have to pay for these services? Neither we nor our partners can afford them. It's difficult enough finding resources to fight poverty, much less a thug. I'm responsible to our patrons."

"What if we paid for the expense?"

"Never. Protect all of the children and the women in Kamathipura. Not me."

"You would rather let yourself be killed then? What about your project?"

"Who wants to kill me? We have had a couple of scares, but they could have been made by neighbors' sons. No one has put a gun to my head."

"Of course," the inspector said. "And the day they do, it will be too late."

I doubted whether these men were truly concerned about my safety. "Moreover," I added, "it is true that my project includes many children of the streets, but they still are few compared to the number of children exploited or killed by the same people you claim are threatening to kill me. Do you really think I am important to them?"

"The children benefiting from your project are of no importance to those people, it's true; they have enough children to choose from. But, frankly, they care even less about your life."

The inspector seemed honest and his words rattled me. That night I couldn't sleep.

Soon I came to accept the threats as real. I agreed to a bodyguard only after my father, grandmother, friends, and colleagues implored me to accept protection. I registered at the embassy (which I hadn't done in the three years I had been living in Bombay): if anything happened they could contact the appropriate people. And so I had to become accustomed to going out with a bodyguard. He had to inspect places I was planning to visit, scrutinize people surrounding me, know which employees were authorized to enter my office, who my neighbors were, and so on.

The bottom of my car was always checked with a little mirror before I got in. Very often such measures were awkward. I was ashamed. I arrived at meetings with the need to explain. My lunch companions, for example, always noted and commented on the security, which I tried to explain and which then became the topic of conversation for the rest of the meal. I found the entire process disruptive.

Fortunately, the security team was discreet. Nevertheless, my table at restaurants had to be approved; often I was segregated. Many routine activities were no longer allowed: no more rickshaw trips without protection, and so on. I was getting used to the restrictions, but there were exceptions.

"You shouldn't stroll casually in the slum areas," a guard said to me one day when we were in Dharavi.

"Look, you are supposed to protect my life," I responded. "If you don't allow me near the poor then my life will not have to be protected, because you will have killed me. They are my life. If you take me away from them you will be taking away the meaning of my life. And so, please, I will continue to meet with them, and I will continue to spend day in and day out in these shacks. They are the ones who protect me. I assure you that nothing will happen inside these districts. How can I be afraid for my life when there are so many people protecting me with gratitude? I have given them my life. It is entirely in their hands. Do you think they wouldn't protect me?"

One day my good friend Oscar Capella, who was visiting from Barcelona, accompanied me to the slums. I was ashamed of the security, of the feeling of the lack of liberty.

"Look Jaume," said Oscar, trying to cheer me up, "just think about it as something normal, like having to wait in a restaurant before being seated. Think about all this as the same kind of thing."

Some amusing events occurred during those days with Oscar. There was a huge commotion when the elevator we had taken got stuck between floors. I had "escaped" from the bodyguards, and was scolded later that day. As with most things, one gets used to guards, as do the people in one's life.

The Price of Love

I REMEMBER WITH CLARITY the days and months after my mother's death. We never lost hope during her struggle, but she died on February 10, 1996. I heard the word "overcome" a lot during the following days: "You must overcome it," "These things have to be overcome," "One never overcomes something like this" and so on.

What does it mean, to "overcome" death? If overcome means to forget, none of our family wanted to do so. If overcome means being able to talk about her and smile, then we had already overcome it that same day, because her memory was, and is, alive with us. Several books about death circulated in my home around that time. I especially remember *Death: The Final Stage of Growth* by Elisabeth Kübler-Ross, an interesting book given to me by my grandmother Martha. The author explains how death is the culmination of our living experiences, its crowning, what gives meaning and value to our lives. Without life there would not be death, but without death there would not be life either. I have met many people who are or have been very close to death, and they all get the most out of life, like someone who sees death as something external and far away.

In order to really appreciate life, one has to learn not to ignore death but to know it is there, like one more process in our lives. The possibility of having something happen that would end my visit to this world is painful, because I would miss my loved ones, but it's not worrisome.

This fight called Bombay Smiles will continue after I am gone. No one is indispensable. When that isn't the case, the project has been badly thought out.

SMILES OF AN
UNFORESEEN DESTINY

> An individual is separated, cut away. An individual
> is a separate entity, without relationships. A person
> is an individual with relationships. If you are
> one with others, if you live for others, you widen
> yourself. —SWAMI VIVEKANANDA

Many people who have written to me from Spain and other places in the world have congratulated me for my courage. I believe most human beings, finding themselves in the situation in which I found myself, would act similarly. Humanity is the prize we receive for such actions, and we are all part of humanity; we are all human. Others have reproached me and still do, for losing my personal identity, for excessively denying my individuality, my individual life, and for acquiring a strong and rooted sense of duty for this cause, an over-developed sense of duty, if you will. I don't believe that I am negating myself. On the contrary, I am affirming what I am—because one grows only when one thinks of others, as a citizen and as an inhabitant of the world.

Bombay's needy are not a job; they are a life option, one that I chose freely, without reservation or restraint, without condition. Those who do not understand this do not grasp the concept of giving oneself to others, and how beautiful it can be. To go through life without the pleasure of giving without expecting anything in return is like passing near a crystalline sea without wanting to touch the water.

The world would be very different if we all discovered that the purpose of life is to give unconditionally. So much chronic dissatisfaction would disappear. So much spiritual emptiness would evaporate. So many expressions of love and affection would flower within humanity. There are millions of people chatting in Internet cafés around the world; millions of people sitting in cubicles with only a computer in sight. They spend a great deal of time trying to present themselves to the world, trying to meet people. Meanwhile they ignore their customers and their colleagues. Wouldn't it be more sensible, more enriching, to turn off their computers and go have a cup of coffee with one another?

People are immersed in a collective blindness; when, for some reason, they suddenly open their eyes, it is their own sufferings and needs that they notice. To love, one must love oneself, be happy with oneself. Our own emptiness cannot be filled by others; volume must emerge from within. And it's only then that one can help others, that one can exude happiness which acts as a gravitational force on others, which is beneficial to others. Our happiness is then like a clear crystal, untainted; if the crystal is foggy or dirty, it rarely projects light.

It is necessary to think about helping from the perspective of the one being helped and never from the point of view of the one who helps. That feeling, called "charity" by some, and by others "cooperation," must be a search for the happiness of the one being helped, never the search for one's own happiness. Our own happiness will come; it will flow by itself amid that beautiful harmony that always appears when one acts with one's heart. But one must not look for it in other people's weaknesses. That is a mistake.

I receive many letters from people who want to come to India to "find themselves." One doesn't need to travel halfway around the world to find oneself; it's there, in our own backyards—in our hearts, much closer than we think.

Just as a doctor needs to see a patient to properly diagnose that patient, so we must see our souls in order to cure them. It is necessary to observe the soul the way one would watch the imperfect movements of a baby, with empathy, with understanding. Once we *see* ourselves, we discover one of the greatest treasures in the world: that we belong where we are, which is that we belong everywhere. We will know that we are a part of the universe and the universe is part of us; one and the other. Is it not marvelous to discover that we are a part of the same material with which stars, the crystal clear water of rivers, and sunsets are embroidered? The discovery of that secret and the understanding that follows cannot be bought. That knowledge is, with love, the largest treasure that we possess in our souls.

Originally, I arrived in Bombay looking for nothing. But I found everything. I found the happiness of many people. I found my own. My destiny smiled at me and gave me the world—beginning with a touch, the touch of the friendly hands of the untouchables, as they are unjustly called. The warmth of their eyes and the love of their souls followed.

I am happy to know that I am in a city where I can help others in a modest way. I am happy because they live and I live with them. I am happy because I see the possibilities of their futures, the biggest goal of my happiness and the true sense of my life.

Bombay struck my soul with such force that I crossed the limits of my own destiny. And then that destiny shook me out of my complacency. I then understood that Bombay contained the rest of my life. Like other cities, it is teeming with imperfections and injustice, yet I love it with all my soul and all my heart.

As I wrote earlier, one of the first beneficiaries of Bombay Smiles, on the first day of Spanish class, wrote on the blackboard that "God has rewarded us with Jaume." It would take many blackboards to capture the scope of how much the children of Bombay have given me. There have been obstacles. There will be more. Nothing of excellence is easy; anything easy lacks excellence. If you devote your life to the pursuit of a dream, life will turn that dream to reality, with interest. And if that dream is dedicated to others, the wind will always be at your back.

This is the story of how I found the wind always at my back.

Bombay Smiles, the NGO founded by Jaume Sanllorente in 2004, currently provides jobs for more than 300 people in India. The project has directly benefited the lives of some of the most disadvantaged people there, including those in the untouchables caste and patients with leprosy. Bombay Smiles addresses five broad areas: education, families, leprosy awareness, medical expeditions, and job creation.

Today, Bombay Smiles continues to be Jaume Sanllorente's dream for offering dignity and the possibility of a better future to the most disadvantaged residents of Mumbai.

If you are interested in becoming a sponsor or making a donation, or if you'd simply like to learn more about the work of Bombay Smiles, please visit www.bombaysmiles.org or email usa@bombaysmiles.org.